30-SECOND
ANCIENT GREECE

30-SECOND
ANCIENT GREECE

THE 50 MOST IMPORTANT ACHIEVEMENTS OF A TIMELESS
CIVILIZATION, EACH EXPLAINED IN HALF A MINUTE

Editor
Matthew Nicholls

Contributors
Emma Aston
Timothy Duff
Patrick Finglass
Katherine Harloe
Matthew Nicholls
Kelli Rudolph
Amy C. Smith

Illustrator
Nicky Ackland-Snow

IVY PRESS

This paperback edition published in the UK in 2018 by
Ivy Press
An imprint of The Quarto Group
The Old Brewery, 6 Blundell Street
London N7 9BH, United Kingdom
T (0)20 7700 6700 **F** (0)20 7700 8066
www.QuartoKnows.com

First published in hardback in 2016

© 2017 Quarto Publishing plc

British Library Cataloguing-in-
Publication Data
A CIP catalogue record for this
book is available from the
British Library

ISBN: 978-1-78240-590-0

This book was conceived,
designed and produced by
Ivy Press
58 West Street, Brighton BN1 2RA, UK

Publisher **Susan Kelly**
Creative Director **Michael Whitehead**
Editorial Director **Tom Kitch**
Commissioning Editor **Sophie Collins**
Project Editor **Joanna Bentley**
Designer **Ginny Zeal**
Picture Researcher **Katie Greenwood**
Illustrator **Nicky Ackland-Snow**
Glossaries Text **Matthew Nicholls**

Printed in China

10 9 8 7 6 5 4 3 2 1

CONTENTS

INTRODUCTION
Matthew Nicholls

The ancient Greeks thought of themselves as

linked by language, religion and a complex web of ethnic and political ties, but they did not inhabit a nation state: the world that emerged from the Greek dark ages by around 800 BCE was a fragmented landscape of individual, competing city states (*polis*, plural *poleis*). These *poleis* filled the peninsula and islands of modern Greece, often competing over its limited agricultural land, but were also found across the Aegean Sea on the coast of Asia Minor (modern Turkey) and in cities as far away as southern Italy and even France. Their capacity for both shared cultural identity and intense mutual competition spurred an extraordinarily fertile creative energy.

Alexander the Great's lightning conquests spread Greek culture further afield than ever before, ushering in the Hellenistic period.

The 'Greek miracle' of the Archaic and Classical periods, around 800–300 BCE, marked a profound moment in the development of civilization. The Greeks made huge strides in almost every field of human endeavour. They were enormously interested in the power of the spoken and written word, developing new literary forms (epic and lyric poetry, drama, history), which they wrote down with an alphabet developed through contact with the Levant. They experimented with new ways of organizing their societies (democracy, oligarchy, different sorts of empire, jury trials, the power of rhetoric), and they thought about these deeply and systematically. They enquired profoundly into the human condition through literature, philosophy, artistic representation (in painting, pottery and sculpture), and even sport. They built dramatic new architectural settings for these activities, from theatres and gymnasia to spectacular temples.

This period of intense development reached one high-water mark in Athens during the fifth to fourth centuries BCE, and much of our evidence is from this remarkable city. In many ways the achievements of Athens' 'Classical' period – its architecture, sculpture, philosophy, drama and democracy – are what come to mind when we think of the ancient Greeks.

The 'Panhellenic' festivals of the ancient Greek world would often feature music and drama as well as athletics, wrestling and boxing, and were the inspiration for the modern Olympic Games.

But Athens was one among many competing Greek *poleis*, and as its star faded, other centres of power – Thebes, Macedon, Alexandria – rose to prominence. The world of small, competing city-states (and Athens' two centuries of experimentation with democracy) was disrupted by the ambition and resources of autocratic rulers who built larger, hegemonic power blocks. The greatest of these was the Macedonian Alexander the Great, whose conquests radically expanded the boundaries of the Greek world. The 'Hellenistic' kingdoms that succeeded his empire continued to spread Greek ideas across the Middle East, explaining why the greatest library of the Greek world was found in Egyptian Alexandria, and why Greek architectural forms are found as far away as modern Afghanistan.

In time the Hellenistic kingdoms themselves fell to invasion as Rome eclipsed the political, but not the cultural, power of its Greek neighbours. Greek thought continued to exert a powerful influence over the Roman imagination; Rome took many of its gods, literary forms, architectural styles and artistic treasures from the Greeks. Today the influence of Greek ideas is felt in almost every sphere of intellectual and cultural life, in politics, economics, rhetoric, philosophy, democracy, technology, mathematics, drama and music – all terms derived from Greek words. As Shelley wrote in the preface to his drama *Hellas*, 'We are all Greeks. Our laws, our literature, our religion, our arts have their root in Greece.'

Stone-cut inscriptions that survive in many Greek sites tell historians a great deal about life in the ancient past.

An overview of Greek history

The map shows the eastern Mediterranean with the following labels:

THRACE · Byzantium · Sea of Marmara · PROPONTIS · MACEDONIA · THASOS · SAMOTHRACE · IMBROS · LEMNOS · Troy · EPIRUS · CORCYRA · Dodona · THESSALY · Pergamum · ASIA MINOR · Sardis · Thermopylae · EUBOEA · SCYRUS · LESBOS · ITHACA · Delphi · BOEOTIA · Gulf of Corinth · Thebes · Marathon · CHIOS · Smyrna · CEPHALLANIA · ACHAEA · ATTICA · Piraeus · Athens · ANDROS · Ephesus · ZACYNTHOS · Olympia · Corinth · Mycenae · SALAMIS · SAMOS · IKAROS · Miletus · Argos · TENOS · PELOPONNESE · KYTHNOS · Pylos · Sparta · SERIPHOS · NAXOS · Halicarnassus · SIPHNOS · MELOS · THERA · Cnidus · CYTHERA · RHODES · CRETE · Knossos

The eastern Mediterranean in the fifth century BCE. Greek city-states or poleis spread across the mainland, the islands of the Aegean Sea, and beyond.

ca. 1575 BCE onwards
Mycenaean Greek civilization dominant in Greece and Aegean

ca. 1425–1200 BCE
Linear B used to write Mycenaean Greek

ca. 1200 BCE
Wave of civilizational collapses in the eastern Mediterranean, including Mycenaean Greeks, Hittites in Anatolia and Syria, and the new kingdom in Egypt

ca. 1200–800 BCE
Greek 'dark ages'

8th century BCE
Development of the Greek alphabet

776 BCE
Traditional date for first Olympic games

ca. 750–725 BCE
Possible dates for the *Iliad* and the *Odyssey*, epic poems traditionally attributed to Homer

8th–7th century BCE
Greek *polis* city states grow, send out daughter colonies, experiment with different political forms and make war with one another

Late 7th century BCE
Sappho writes poems on the island of Lesbos

594/3 BCE
Influential lawgiver Solon is chief magistrate at Athens

ca. 570 BCE
Birth of Pythagoras

507 BCE
Athenian reformer Cleisthenes comes to prominence in Athens; begins democratic reforms

490 BCE
Persian King Darius' attack on Athens fails after Athenian victory at Marathon

484 BCE
Aeschlyus wins the first of his 13 prizes for tragedy at Athenian Dionysia dramatic festival

480–79 BCE
Persian King Xerxes' invasion of Greece fails: the Spartans delay the Persians at Thermopylae, and the Greeks defeat them by sea at Salamis and on land at Plataea

478/7 BCE
Athens forms her Delian League against the Persians, laying the foundations for three quarters of a century of dominance

468 BCE
Sophocles wins his first prize for tragedy at the Dionysia

ca. 461–429 BCE
Athenian democracy (and empire) established; career of Pericles

447–432 BCE
Construction and decoration of Parthenon at Athens

441 BCE
Euripides wins his first prize for tragedy at the Dionysia

431–404 BCE
Peloponnesian War between Athens and Sparta, ending in defeat for Athens

428 BCE
Birth of Plato

427 BCE
First production of a comedy by Aristophanes

411, 404 BCE
Harsh oligarchic regimes replace Athens' democracy

399 BCE
Execution of Socrates

384 BCE
Birth of Aristotle

336 BCE
Alexander the Great succeeds his father Philip II of Macedon

323 BCE
Death of Alexander after conquest of much of the eastern Mediterranean and Middle East

Late 4th century BCE
Alexander's empire splits into Hellenistic kingdoms ruled by competing generals

Early 3rd century BCE
Foundation of the library at Alexandria

214–148 BCE
Series of 'Macedonian' wars between Rome and various Greek kingdoms for control of the eastern Mediterranean

146 BCE
Sack of Corinth and Carthage – Rome controls much of Greece and the Mediterranean

31 BCE
Battle of Actium – Rome defeats Hellenistic Ptolemy dynasty and conquers Egypt

1st–2nd centuries CE
Period of renewed prosperity and cultural achievement for Greek provinces under Roman rule

285 CE
Roman emperor Diocletian splits the empire into eastern (Greek) and western halves

330 CE
Christian Roman emperor Constantine moves the capital of the empire to Byzantium (Constantinople)

1453 CE
Final fall of Byzantium

How this book works

The seven chapters of this book aim to explore the rich history and legacy of the ancient Greeks. The breadth of the subject matter here reflects the wide range of their achievements, and the way in which these are studied in universities around the world. Classicists, linguists, historians, archaeologists, philosophers and art historians all study the world of the ancient Greeks, working with very different bodies of material, questions and approaches. Compressing this rich field of study into only 50 entries was a challenge.

The first chapter, **The Greek World**, gives an overview of the main powers in the Greek world and the outline of Greek history from the Classical age of the fifth century BCE to the advent of Rome. It will work particularly well if you have read through this introduction and its timeline. **People & Society** explores Greek society, from the polarities between Greek and non-Greek, and between citizen, non-citizen and slave, to the common institutions of civic life and law that governed their communities and the important world of agriculture. **Myth & Religion** introduces us both to the gods and heroes of Greek belief, and to the ways in which they were worshipped. **Literature** gives the briefest of introductions to Greek literature and its chief figures, genre by genre – epic and lyric poetry, tragic and comic drama, prose history and oratory, and philosophy. These short entries can only give you an introduction, and I would be delighted if any readers of this book were motivated to go and read the works of some of these wonderful authors (the histories of Herodotus would be a good starting point). **Language & Learning** expands this look at Greek literary endeavour by considering the nature of the Greek language, how it was written down and circulated, and what intellectual achievements it recorded. There follow two chapters on the famous **Architecture & Buildings** of the Greeks, from temples to townhouses, and their **Arts**, including painted vases, various ages of sculpture, painting, metalwork and jewellery.

Greek vases were often painted with figures from myths and legends and images from daily life.

Warfare was a recurrent feature of Greek life, making a mark on much Greek art and literature.

The chapters in the book, and the individual entries, can be read one after another or can be dipped into at random. The main text gives an overview of the topic at hand. The accompanying 3-second survey offers a quick synopsis, while a separate paragraph, the 3-minute excavation, provides a different angle on the subject, some more information, or a point to think about.

Each chapter has a glossary to help with unfamiliar terminology and concepts, and a central biographical profile relevant to the chapter's overall theme. Picking the subjects for these was an interesting challenge. Some figures – Homer, Alexander the Great – were impossible to leave out, but I also wanted to pick some who cast a different light on Greek society, the evidence for which very often preserves the outlook of high-status Greek men. So instead of Pericles (who appears in other chapters) we feature his non-Athenian mistress, Aspasia; Sappho gives us a female contribution to the largely male world of Greek literature; and Zeus, whose biography is to say the least unconventional, introduces us to the dysfunctional family of the Olympian gods.

I hope that this cast of characters, and the 50 entries in this book, will give readers a glimpse into the fascinating, turbulent and creative world of the ancient Greeks.

Statesmen like Pericles helped Athens to greatness in the fifth century BCE.

THE GREEK WORLD

THE GREEK WORLD
GLOSSARY

Achaean League Federal organization of cities in the Greek region of Achaea, which lasted in various forms until the region fell to Rome in the mid second century BCE.

acropolis Literally 'upper city': a high point within a *polis*, often fortified as a citadel and acting as a nucleus or strongpoint housing important civic and/or religious buildings.

agora A central open area within the *polis* where people gathered informally (e.g. for commerce) and sometimes for certain formal political activities; often lined, as at Athens, with important civic buildings.

Antigonids Dynasty of Hellenistic kings descending from Alexander the Great's general Antigonus Monophthalmus ('one-eyed'). They ruled over Macedon and much of mainland Greece until their eventual defeat by Rome in 168 BCE.

Archaic period (ca. eighth to early fifth century BCE.) A phase of Greek history in which distinctive phenomena started to emerge as the dark ages came to an end – *polis* states (including daughter colonies), the alphabet, Panhellenic sanctuaries and their festivals, new artistic forms, and increased prosperity and trade.

Asia Minor Latin name for the peninsula occupied by modern Turkey, between the Aegean, the Black Sea and the Euphrates. Though the heartland was part of the Persian Empire from ca. 546 BCE until the conquests of Alexander, many Greeks settled on its western coast from ca. 1100 BCE. Eventually these cities developed into great centres of Greek culture, such as Ephesus.

black-figure pottery Technique for decorating pottery developed from the eighth century BCE. Silhouette-like figures were painted on to the red clay of the vessel, and their details picked out by engraved lines.

Boeotian League Confederacy of *poleis* from the central Greek region of Boeotia, linked by common cultural, religious and linguistic characteristics.

Carthage A city in present-day Tunisia: founded by Phoenician colonists, it grew to be head of a great maritime empire that rivaled Rome for control of the Mediterranean.

Delphi One of the four great Panhellenic sanctuaries sacred to all the Greeks. Home of the famous and influential oracle of Apollo and of the Pythian Games in Apollo's honour.

Hellespont Greek name for the Dardanelles Strait, a vital route separating Europe from Asia and leading from the Aegean via the Sea of Marmara to the Black Sea.

hoplite Heavy infantryman, the 'standard' soldier of the *polis*. Armed with spear and sword, and defended by helmet and shield.

Mesopotamia From the Greek for 'between the rivers': the land between the Tigris and Euphrates river systems, stretching south-east through parts of modern Syria, Iraq and Iran. Part of the Persian Empire until its invasion by Alexander.

Olympia A Panhellenic sanctuary site. Sacred to Zeus and home of the Olympic games, where athletes from all over the Greek world gathered to compete every four years in August or September.

Panhellenic Literally of 'all the Greeks'. Used especially of the four great Panhellenic sanctuaries (Delphi, Olympia, Nemea and Isthmia) whose games were open to all Greeks, but also of the broader idea that Greeks, even those at war with one another, shared characteristics in common that marked them off from non-Greeks.

province Territorial subdivision of the Roman empire, administered by a governor appointed in Rome.

Ptolemies The ruling dynasty of Hellenistic Egypt. Founded at the death of Alexander the Great by his general Ptolemy (King Ptolemy I, 323–283 BCE), they ruled down to the defeat and suicide (in 30 BCE) of Cleopatra, last of the Ptolemies, at the hands of the future Roman emperor Augustus.

Seleucids Dynasty who ruled a huge and fluctuating swathe of the former empire of Alexander the Great, from central Turkey through Syria to Iran and central Asia. Founded by Alexander's former general Seleucus I Nicator (305–281 BCE), they ruled down to Antiochus XIII Asiaticus, who was deposed by the Roman general Pompey the Great in 64 BCE.

Sogdian Coming from Sogdia, a region in modern day Uzbekistan and Tajikistan.

thetes The lowest economic class of free citizen males in Athens.

THE *POLIS*

the 30-second history

There was no single state or government to which all Greeks owed loyalty. Instead, the Greek world comprised about 1,500 small autonomous city-states (*poleis*), often at war with each other. Each *polis* was a self-governing community, and its territory consisted of a rural hinterland and an urban centre usually containing temples, a public meeting place or *agora*, a theatre and an *acropolis*. The population of a *polis* was usually under 10,000, sometimes scarcely more than a thousand. Athens, with a population of several hundred thousand, and Sparta with a territory bigger than Athens, were exceptional. Most *poleis* shared certain key institutions: an assembly of citizens, which had some decision-making power, a smaller council and annual officials. But *poleis* differed in the power accorded to the citizen assembly and the breadth of its membership. Many *poleis* were entirely independent; some were in a dependent relationship with larger neighbours. Alliances and wars between *poleis* were frequent, and in some regions *poleis* pooled sovereignty to form federal states, such as the Boeotian, or later Achaean, Leagues. The rise of Macedonia, the conquests of Alexander the Great, the formation of the Hellenistic kingdoms and finally Roman domination all posed problems for the *poleis*, but they survived to the end of antiquity and beyond.

3-SECOND SURVEY
The Greek world was divided into hundreds of *poleis*, or city-states, which were self-governing communities based round an urban centre.

3-MINUTE EXCAVATION
The philosopher Aristotle's work *Politics* ('*polis*- matters'), written ca. 330 BCE, examines the form of government and institutions which he thought would best enable the citizens of a *polis* to live a happy life. He famously said that 'man was by nature an animal of the *polis*' and claimed that ideally a *polis* should have few enough citizens for everyone to know each other and be able to gather together in one place.

RELATED HISTORIES
See also
'FROGS AROUND A POND'
page 24

POLITICS & DEMOCRACY
page 38

CITIZENS
page 42

CIVIC ARCHITECTURE
page 130

3-SECOND BIOGRAPHY
ARISTOTLE
384–322 BCE
Philosopher resident in Athens, author of a vast number of works on political theory, ethics, natural science and more

30-SECOND TEXT
Timothy Duff

The Acropolis in Athens was at the heart of one of the greatest Greek poleis, or city-states.

ATHENS & SPARTA

the 30-second history

Sparta and Athens were the two

great powers of fifth-century BCE Greece. Initially allies against Persia, they fought each other in the Peloponnesian War for much of the second half of the century. Literature of the time (usually by Athenians) portrays the two cities as opposites: Athens a varied and vigorous democracy which maintained its political power by means of its fleet; Sparta an oligarchy which kept strict control over every aspect of its citizens' lives, ruled its serf population with an iron fist and relied on the might of its land army. Yet some Athenian writers, such as Plato and Xenophon, admired Sparta for the stability and longevity of her political constitution, known as *eunomia* or 'good order'. Spartan soldiers were a byword for bravery, Spartan women for beauty and wit. But Sparta is most famous for its communal way of life: a few thousand citizen men, trained for military service and unproductive economically, who lived and dined in common and whose everyday needs were serviced by a larger number of *perioeci* ('dwellers-around') and *helots* ('serfs'). These arrangements were attributed to legendary lawgiver, Lycurgus; modern scholars see them as a response to the troubles of governing the Spartan territories of Laconia and Messenia over the Archaic period.

3-SECOND SURVEY
Sparta and Athens, the two leading Greek city-states of the fifth century, fought a war from 431 to 404 BCE that caused the eclipse of Athenian power.

3-MINUTE EXCAVATION
'Laconic speech' and a 'Spartan lifestyle' are phrases that bear witness to enduring stereotypes of Sparta. But were the Spartans really people of little luxury and few words? The imbalance of our sources, most of which are Athenian, makes reconstructing the society of Athens' greatest rival a difficult task. Black-figure pottery and the choral lyrics of Alcman attest to the importance of Spartan cultural production and provide a corrective to later Athenian caricatures.

RELATED HISTORIES
See also
PERSIAN & PELOPONNESIAN WARS
page 20

WARFARE
page 22

GREEKS & BARBARIANS
page 36

3-SECOND BIOGRAPHIES
PERICLES
ca. 495–429 BCE
Statesman and general who led Athens into the Peloponnesian War

LEONIDAS
ruled ca. 490–480 BCE
King of Sparta, led the troops at Thermopylae defending Greece from Persian invaders

GORGO
fl. 480 BCE
Wife of Leonidas

30-SECOND TEXT
Katherine Harloe

Sparta, with its famous army, and maritime Athens were the two great Greek powers of the fifth century BCE.

PERSIAN & PELOPONNESIAN WARS

the 30-second history

During the sixth century BCE,

the Greek cities of Asia Minor came under Persian rule. The Persian Wars began when Athens sent ships to support the unsuccessful revolt of these cities from Persia (499–494 BCE). A Persian force sent to punish Athens was then defeated at the Battle of Marathon in 490. Ten years later, the Persians launched a massive invasion with the intention of annexing all the mainland Greek states. Against the odds, an alliance led by Greece's foremost military power, Sparta, defeated the Persians by sea at Salamis (480) and on land at Plataea (479). The Greek cities of Asia Minor were soon liberated from Persian control. Athens, which had provided the largest navy, soon found itself at the head of a naval alliance, the Delian League, which aimed at preventing Persian encroachments. But in the five decades that followed, Athens gradually turned this alliance into her own empire. Finally, Sparta and her allies in the Peloponnese attacked Athens in 431. The Peloponnesian War lasted 27 years; Sparta was unable to strike a decisive blow while Athens controlled the seas, and Athens was unable to face the Spartans in battle on land. The stalemate was only broken when Sparta quietly agreed to cede Asia Minor to Persia in return for huge financial subsidies: it was Persian gold that won the war.

3-SECOND SURVEY
Athens and Sparta were allies in the Persian Wars, but less than 50 years later fought each other in the Peloponnesian War.

3-MINUTE EXCAVATION
Thucydides argued that the 'truest cause' of the Peloponnesian War was not the immediate flashpoints which sparked it off, but Sparta's fear of Athens' growing power, which they felt had to be destroyed before it was too late. Athens' eventual surrender in 404 BCE left Sparta completely dominant in Greece. But Sparta bullied and fell out with her allies, and within less than 40 years she too had been eclipsed.

RELATED HISTORIES
See also
ATHENS & SPARTA
page 18

WARFARE
page 22

'FROGS AROUND A POND'
page 24

3-SECOND BIOGRAPHIES
HERODOTUS
ca. 485–ca. 424 BCE
A Greek from Halicarnassus in Asia Minor, who wrote a history of the Persian Wars

THUCYDIDES
born ca. 460 BCE
An Athenian commander, author of a long work on the Peloponnesian War

30-SECOND TEXT
Timothy Duff

The clash between the Persian and Greek states led to battles on land and at sea.

WARFARE

the 30-second history

Warfare was almost constant

in ancient Greek life, both in famous conflicts such as the Persian and Peloponnesian Wars and in the perennial low-level bickering between neighbouring states over land and other local grievances. The destructive aspects of war were recognized; even in Homer's *Iliad*, a poem in which battle confers heroic glory, the war-god Ares is a hated figure. But there was no universal ideology of pacifism: violent conflict was simply accepted as a fact of life. Moreover, in the *polis*, every citizen was, on the face of it, a soldier. Warfare was not the preserve of professionals: fighting for one's state was one of the obligations of citizenship, and there were few professional standing armies. In most regions, the citizen-soldier *par excellence* was the hoplite, the heavily armed infantryman who, shoulder to shoulder with his comrades, formed the core of the typical battle-formation and embodied the ideal of social cooperation. Hoplite warfare emerged as early as the eighth century BCE, but it was in the fifth that it came to dominate both the practicalities and the ideology of the battlefield. Other types of soldier played subsidiary roles: the cavalry was used to harry the enemy's flanks and to pursue him in rout; archers and slingers could help to weaken the opposing line. However, the hoplite was the core of both army and polis.

3-SECOND SURVEY
The hoplite – a heavily armed foot-soldier – dominated Classical Greek warfare, not only on the battlefield but also as the symbolic embodiment of the cooperative citizen.

3-MINUTE EXCAVATION
The close relationship between military and political life can be seen in Athens' famous navy. Athens' military supremacy in the 5th century BCE depended upon control of the sea and the commercial shipping lanes. The rowers in the Athenian ships were *thetes* – the poorest class in the city, who could not afford hoplite armour – and it was their vital contribution to war and security that led to their enfranchisement as citizens. So the famous Athenian democracy was in part a product of her naval power.

3-SECOND BIOGRAPHY
TYRTAEUS
late seventh century BCE
Spartan poet whose description of brave fighters locking shields against the foe is the perfect evocation of hoplite values

30-SECOND TEXT
Emma Aston

The hoplite was the essential figure of Greek warfare on land.

'FROGS AROUND A POND'

the 30-second history

3-SECOND SURVEY
The Greeks rarely settled far inland. Socrates compared the people of the known world 'to frogs or ants round a pond', i.e. the Mediterranean.

3-MINUTE EXCAVATION
The *poleis* of mainland Greece formed only a small part of the Greek world and were not necessarily the most wealthy; their concerns were not always shared by Greeks elsewhere. While mainland cities were fighting the Persian Wars, others in Sicily were resisting Carthaginian invasion. Cities in Asia Minor were, until Alexander's conquest, frequently under Persian control, while those in Italy, North Africa or the Black Sea had to deal with very different local conditions.

From their heartland in the

mainland of Greece, the Greeks had, by the end of the Archaic period, settled round the shores of the Mediterranean and the Black Sea in one of the greatest colonizing movements in history. Greek *poleis* peppered the coast from Spain and Provence to Sicily, southern Italy, North Africa, the Levant, Asia Minor and as far north as Crimea. In founding cities so far afield the Greeks inevitably came into contact with numerous other peoples, from the ancient cultures of Persia and Egypt, the latter of which the Greeks considered far older than their own, to tribal societies in the Balkans, Celts in the west, Etruscans and Romans in Italy, and many more. Intermarriage and assimilation led to a diversity of Greek cultures, but Greek *poleis* shared a common language and common customs, and even far-flung colonial foundations, though independent, kept up ties with their mother cities. Many Greek *poleis* sent representatives to compete in athletic competitions or made dedications at the great Panhellenic religious sanctuaries at Delphi and Olympia, which formed a focal point for the whole Greek-speaking world. While overland travel and trade was difficult and expensive, the sea connected rather than divided the numerous Greek cities.

RELATED HISTORIES
See also
THE *POLIS*
page 16

GREEKS & BARBARIANS
page 36

TRADE & THE ECONOMY
page 52

PANHELLENIC FESTIVALS
page 70

3-SECOND BIOGRAPHY
SOCRATES
ca. 470/469–399 BCE
Athenian philosopher, known for his questioning style; executed, but immortalized in the writing of his pupils, Plato, Xenophon and others

30-SECOND TEXT
Timothy Duff

Greek settlements spread along the coasts of the Mediterranean and beyond, linked by ties of language and religion.

356 BCE
Alexander born. Later tutored by Aristotle

336 BCE
His father Philip is assassinated. Alexander becomes king of Macedonia

334 BCE
Invades Persian territory in Asia Minor. Battle of Granicus

333 BCE
Defeats Persian king Darius at Issus. Alexander advances through Phoenicia

332 BCE
Welcomed in Egypt as a liberator

331 BCE
Founds Alexandria. Defeats Darius at Gaugamela in Mesopotamia

330–327 BCE
Campaigns in Central Asia

327 BCE
Invades India (modern Pakistan), which is beyond the eastern frontiers of the Persian Empire

326 BCE
Defeats Porus, an Indian ruler, but his army mutinies and refuses to go further

323 BCE
Alexander returns to Babylon, contracts fever and dies. His generals soon fall to fighting amongst themselves

ALEXANDER

Alexander the Great changed western history. He became King of Macedonia, a large fertile region in northern Greece, at the age of 20, when his father Philip II was assassinated. He inherited from Philip a united kingdom, a professional and experienced army and *de facto* control of most cities of mainland Greece. After suppressing trouble on his northern borders and the revolt of Thebes, he crossed the Hellespont and invaded Persian-held territory in Asia Minor. In a series of brilliant campaigns, he advanced down the coast, taking key cities, and finally defeated the Persian king Darius and his huge army at Issus in what is now southern Turkey. He was greeted in Egypt as a liberator and founded Alexandria, before plunging eastwards into Mesopotamia, winning a decisive battle at Gaugamela and taking Babylon.

From this point onwards, Alexander began to behave as Darius' successor and reappointed Persian and local officials to key posts rather than simply imposing Macedonian or Greek officers. To the disgust of some of his officers, he also adopted items of Persian dress and court etiquette. He continued his advance eastwards, through modern Iran, Afghanistan and beyond, and only halted when his troops mutinied in Pakistan and he had to turn back.

Alexander's success in conquering the mighty Persian Empire astounded observers at the time. His personal charisma, decisive leadership and courage played a huge part. But the Persian Empire was already weak; major revolts had occurred in the preceding decades. Alexander also had the benefit of his father's newly reformed, professional and highly manoeuvrable army, which included experienced infantry with 6-metre-long (almost 20 feet) pikes, elite cavalry and a formidable expertise in siege warfare.

Alexander's career was cut short when he died of fever in Babylonia at the age of 33, leaving behind him a vast empire, but no obvious heir. His empire quickly fragmented as his generals fought each other for control. However, Alexander's reputation as the greatest conqueror the ancient world had seen has remained intact. Generals and emperors, from Julius Caesar and Pompey to Napoleon, have tried to emulate him and bask in his reflected glory. Our earliest extant sources on Alexander, such as Plutarch's biography, date to several centuries after his death. Most admire him as the archetypal king and general; but some also present him as corrupted by the East, becoming increasingly despotic and prone to rage and drunkenness.

Timothy Duff

HELLENISTIC KINGDOMS

the 30-second history

3-SECOND SURVEY
The Hellenistic kingdoms arose out of Alexander's vast empire after half a century of internecine war that followed his death.

3-MINUTE EXCAVATION
The Hellenistic kingdoms were supranational states, which incorporated within their territory both Greek *poleis* and many non-Greek peoples, ruled over by a Greco-Macedonian elite. The Greek *poleis*, including Athens and Sparta, were now minor players and struggled to maintain their autonomy and remain on good terms with the Hellenistic kings. But Greek became the common language of education, trade, administration and literature throughout the eastern Mediterranean.

When Alexander died at Babylon in 323 BCE, he left behind him a huge empire, stretching from Macedonia in the west to modern Iran and Afghanistan in the east, and including all of Asia Minor, Syria, Mesopotamia, the Levant and Egypt. But he had no heir, except the as yet unborn child of his Sogdian wife. The result was half a century of warfare, as the former generals of Alexander fought across the vast plains of Asia, first for control of the whole empire and then for control of distinct sections of it. Out of these wars were born the Hellenistic kingdoms, each ruled by a Macedonian dynasty descended from one of Alexander's officers (the 'successors'): the Antigonids in Macedonia itself, the Ptolemies in Egypt and the Seleucids in Syria and Babylonia and initially as far as Central Asia. Other smaller kingdoms developed at this time, such as Pergamum, Bithynia, Pontus and Cappadocia in Asia Minor, and Epirus in north-west Greece. The Greek cities, though often autonomous, found themselves under the overlordship of one or more of these usually warring kings. The Hellenistic kingdoms, with their Greek-speaking royal courts and administration, dominated the eastern Mediterranean until they fell one by one to Rome.

RELATED HISTORIES
See also
ALEXANDER
page 26

GREECE IN THE ROMAN WORLD
page 30

THE GREEK LANGUAGE
page 98

3-SECOND BIOGRAPHIES
SELEUCUS
ca. 358–281 BCE
One of Alexander's officers, founded the Seleucid dynasty

PTOLEMY
ca. 367–282 BCE
General under Alexander who founded the Ptolemies

CLEOPATRA
69–30 BCE
The last of the Ptolemies; after her defeat by Rome, Egypt became a Roman province

30-SECOND TEXT
Timothy Duff

After the conquests of Alexander, Macedonian-Greek dynasties ruled distant lands including Egypt.

GREECE IN THE ROMAN WORLD

the 30-second history

The Greek cities in southern Italy and Sicily came into contact with Rome as early as the fourth century BCE, as the Romans gradually expanded their power over the Italian peninsula. By the mid third century the Romans were fighting the Carthaginians in Sicily, and by the end of that century, Roman armies were intervening on the Greek mainland against Macedonia, which was turned into a Roman province. In 146 BCE the Romans sacked Corinth and annexed the rest of the Greek mainland. Octavian's defeat of Cleopatra in 31 BCE and annexation of Egypt marked the effective end of the Hellenistic kingdoms. Roman domination did not, however, spell the end of Greek culture, or of the *polis* and its institutions. Greek cities, though subject to the power of the Roman governor, continued to be autonomous and self-governing, and the Romans underwrote the power of local, Greek, landed elites as long as they maintained the status quo. Indeed, the first two centuries CE were in many ways the high point of Greek prosperity and cultural production; it was at this time that cities received their grandest architecture, and many of the most prolific Greek writers, such as Plutarch, Lucian and Galen, flourished; wealthy Greeks even began entering the Roman Senate and commanding Roman armies.

RELATED HISTORIES
See also
THE *POLIS*
page 16

HELLENISTIC KINGDOMS
page 28

3-SECOND BIOGRAPHIES
PLUTARCH
ca. 45–120 CE
Greek philosopher, essayist and author of a vast biographical work, the *Parallel Lives*

GALEN
129–ca. 216 CE
Philosopher and doctor, originally from Asia Minor but resident in Rome for most of his life

30-SECOND TEXT
Timothy Duff

3-SECOND SURVEY
Rome conquered the Greek world gradually between the third and first centuries BCE. Though subject to Rome, Greek *poleis* retained their autonomy and institutions.

3-MINUTE EXCAVATION
Alexander the Great's conquests had spread the Greek language round the world, and Roman rule did not change this. Governors were sent from Rome, and Roman armies were stationed in frontier provinces. But Greek remained the language of literature, science, administration and trade, in all Roman lands east of the Adriatic Sea. It was also the language of the New Testament, and facilitated the spread of Christianity across the Roman world at this period.

Roman military might, and political power, came to dominate the Greek world, but it continued to produce great monuments and writers like Plutarch.

PEOPLE & SOCIETY

Aegean The sea between mainland Greece and Asia Minor, containing many islands. The Aegean was named after the mythical figure Aegeus, who drowned himself in it in grief at his son Theseus' apparent death.

Attica The territory of Athens, about 930 square miles of large, fertile plains, hills and mountains (largely barren, but with important marble quarries and metal mines), and small river valleys.

chattel slave A slave wholly owned, as property, by a master.

city-state See *polis*

helot Serf-like population of Sparta, held in servile status and used for agricultural labour.

Laurium Area of rich silver mines in south-east Attica. The exploitation of new lodes of silver ore here helped finance the glories of Athens' 'golden age' in the fifth-fourth centuries BCE.

Linear B The script used by Mycenaeans to record their Greek language.

metic A 'resident alien' of a *polis* – free, but not a citizen; perhaps a Greek from another *polis* or a non-Greek who had chosen to settle there temporarily or permanently.

Mycenaean Late Bronze Age civilization in Greece (including the palace centre at Mycenae itself) and the Aegean, dominant from ca. 1575 to ca. 1200 BCE.

oikos Greek word for a house, and a household.

oligarchy Rule by a few (Greek *oligoi*), usually a narrow aristocracy of the wealthiest citizens, excluding the majority of citizens from power.

Phoenician The Phoenician people inhabited a series of coastal city-kingdoms in the Levant, from modern Syria to southern Lebanon (eventually conquered and incorporated into the Greek world by Alexander the Great). They were famous seafarers and merchants, whose most famous overseas colony was Carthage.

***polis* (plural *poleis*)** The *polis*, or city-state (with surrounding territory), was the essential political unit of the ancient Greek world, with its own citizen body and legislative structures.

sophist Intellectual and teacher in subjects including philosophical enquiry and the art of oratorical persuasion.

Spartiates The full citizens of Sparta, who called themselves 'equals'. Raised by the state's famously austere public upbringing, they were at the top of a pyramid of statuses, with helots at the bottom.

symposium Drinking party for Greek citizen males, held in the house. Associated both with a set etiquette and with a wide range of entertainment, from philosophical discussion and poetry to drunkenness and the provision of prostitutes.

tyrant An autocratic ruler of a *polis*. Not necessarily a negative term, especially in pre-Classical Greek history when tyranny was a common form of *polis* government.

GREEKS & BARBARIANS

the 30-second history

3-SECOND SURVEY
The Greeks tended to see mankind as divided into Greeks and barbarians, the latter of whom were inferior and slavish.

3-MINUTE EXCAVATION
Aristotle famously argued that barbarians were 'slaves by nature' – that is naturally suited to being slaves and unsuited to being free. But in practice, Greek views of barbarians were a good deal more nuanced than this. Herodotus dealt with non-Greek cultures in an even-handed way, and a century later, Xenophon used a Persian king as a model of enlightened monarchy in his *Education of Cyrus*. And later, when the Greeks ran up against the Romans, the binary distinction was complicated further.

While never united politically, and often at war with each other, the Greeks thought of themselves as descending from common ancestors and sharing a common language, religious practices and way of life. This sense of selfhood was strengthened by contact with the non-Greek peoples around them, to whom they applied the term *barbaroi*. This term originally implied merely linguistic difference (to Greek ears, non-Greek speakers made a 'bar-bar' sound) but after the stunning victory over the Persian Empire by a handful of Greek cities in 480–479 BCE, it developed a derogatory sense. This dismissive attitude to non-Greeks was no doubt bolstered by the fact that slaves were usually (though not exclusively) non-Greek. This allowed the Greeks to project on to foreigners negative qualities of stupidity, servility, weakness, effeminacy, superstition and much more, while implying that they themselves were intelligent, free, strong, masculine and rational; barbarians, they believed, lived under despotic monarchs, while Greeks ruled themselves. In dividing mankind into two groups – Greek and barbarian – and seeing all barbarians as the same, the Greeks were guilty of 'Hellenocentricism', or judging everything by Greek standards – and 'orientalism', that is, associating the East with negative stereotypes.

RELATED HISTORIES
See also
PERSIAN & PELOPONNESIAN WARS
page 20

'FROGS AROUND A POND'
page 24

SLAVERY
page 48

3-SECOND BIOGRAPHIES
CYRUS II, 'THE GREAT'
ruled ca. 559–530 BCE
King of Persia and founder of the Persian Empire

HERODOTUS
ca. 485–ca. 424 BCE
His history of the Persian Wars is also an ethnographic exploration of the Persians

XENOPHON
born ca. 430 BCE
Athenian who spent most of his life in exile; wrote historical and philosophical works

30-SECOND TEXT
Timothy Duff

'Barbarians' were often looked down on by the Greeks, largely for not being Greek.

POLITICS & DEMOCRACY

the 30-second history

3-SECOND SURVEY
In Greece, political participation was a marker of status, seen as a privilege as much as, or more than, a responsibility.

3-MINUTE EXCAVATION
Tyrannies were rare in Classical Greece, but the figure of the tyrant played a dominant role in the Greek political imagination. Tragedies often represent the downfall of tyrants of the heroic period, such as Oedipus or Agamemnon. The memory of sixth-century tyrants like Polycrates of Samos and Pisistratus of Athens, together with fear of Persia and her 'Great King', probably contributed to ongoing interest in this political figure.

The term 'democracy' derives

from the Greek words *demos* ('people'), and *kratos* ('power'). The first democracy we know of was established in Athens in 508/507 BCE, shortly after the expulsion of the tyrant Hippias. The democratic ideal is one of Athens' most important legacies to the modern world, but Athenian democracy differed from modern democracies in many ways. Most importantly, it was 'direct' rather than 'representative'. All freeborn Athenian adult males over the age of 20 could attend the general assembly (*ecclesia*) to speak and vote on laws and policies. Litigation was heard by large panels of citizen-jurors; candidates for political office were often chosen by lot, were required to account for their actions at the end of their term in office, and could be subject to a vote of exile ('ostracism'). These were all ways of ensuring that particular leaders did not gain too much influence within a system founded on equal power. Democracy was just one of the constitutional forms of Classical Greek cities. More usual was oligarchy, where a smaller group of citizens, often the wealthiest, ruled together. Rarer in the fifth century was 'tyranny', where one man had sole control. Participation in political life was seen as a good in itself; this is why the philosopher Aristotle wrote that 'man is a political animal'.

RELATED HISTORIES
See also
THE *POLIS*
page 16

LAW
page 40

CITIZENS
page 42

SLAVERY
page 48

3-SECOND BIOGRAPHIE
CLEISTHENES
born ca. 565 BCE
Athenian politician, who reorganized the Athenian constitution in 508/7 BCE and is traditionally credited with founding the democracy

PISISTRATUS
died 527 BCE
Tyrant of Athens, reputed for restraint in rule, increasing Athenian power overseas and promoting the arts

30-SECOND TEXT
Katherine Harloe

Greek cities like Athe▮ developed different ways of exercising political power.

LAW

the 30-second history

There was no unified Greek legal system: over the centuries individual cities developed their own laws, yielding eventually to Roman law. In pre-Classical Greek states, kings or judges could give oral judgements according to custom; a 'trial' before people and elders is depicted in the *Iliad*. As literacy emerged, written laws began to codify and fix legal customs. Great 'lawgivers' of the seventh and sixth centuries BCE, Draco and Solon in Athens and Lycurgus in Sparta, developed their states' laws into consistent and comprehensive written systems, an essential foundation for sophisticated Classical societies. Private laws covered matters like inheritance, property ownership and debt, and even what we would now consider criminal offences, with victims relied on to bring a case in the absence of public prosecutors. Public law regulated matters such as the conduct of institutions, officials and priests. Litigants could bring a case before a judge or, in some places, a jury, with witnesses and speeches in defence and prosecution. Athens paid its juries of 200 to 1,500 volunteer citizens chosen by lot, so jury service was popular. Trials were held in public and were sometimes political as well as legal battles, an integral part of the operation of the state.

RELATED HISTORIES
See also
POLITICS & DEMOCRACY
page 38

CITIZENS
page 42

ORATORY
page 88

INSCRIPTIONS
page 106

3-SECOND SURVEY
Law was an essential foundation for the development of sophisticated Classical Greek states, establishing an agreed basis for interactions among their citizens.

3-MINUTE EXCAVATION
Our knowledge of Greek laws comes from inscriptions: permanent public displays of laws inscribed on stone fixed them as the communal basis for society. We also have over a hundred court speeches from Athens. These were preserved as examples of oratory for study, but provide for us a rich source of social history, documenting cases of murder, theft, rape (in cases brought by victims' male guardians), slander and inheritance disputes.

3-SECOND BIOGRAPHIES
SOLON
born ca. 640 BCE
Statesman who set up laws for Athens, inscribing them on revolving pillars for public consultation

LYSIAS
ca. 459–380 BCE
Courtroom speechwriter; 34 of his speeches survive and we know he wrote about 130 more

30-SECOND TEXT
Matthew Nicholls

The rule of law was an essential feature of Greek cities, and often leaves a trace in stone inscriptions.

CITIZENS

the 30-second history

The Greeks invented the concept

of citizenship. Not every inhabitant of a *polis* was necessarily a citizen – that is, a full member of its community. Citizenship, which was hereditary and based usually upon paternal descent, conferred rights to own land and not to be taxed, and was an essential prerequisite for taking part in political decision-making through a popular assembly. It also entailed the duty to fight for the *polis*. Excluded from citizenship were women, foreigners (including Greeks from other cities) and slaves, who possessed no rights and were regarded as mere possessions. Many states had a property qualification, which meant that only citizens of a certain wealth were entitled to attend the assembly or take part in decision-making. Democratic Athens was unusual in allowing all citizens, even the very poorest, to play a full part; the abolition of full democracy there in 322 BCE entailed the imposition of a property qualification. In Sparta, full citizens ('Spartiates') were required to pay contributions to their communal mess halls. Those no longer able to do so lost status and became known as 'inferiors'; as a result, by the fourth century BCE the number of full Spartan citizens had dwindled dangerously. Being a citizen of a *polis* remained an important and privileged status even during the Hellenistic and Roman periods.

3-SECOND SURVEY
Only citizens were full members of the *polis*. Citizenship conferred important rights and privileges unavailable to non-citizens.

3-MINUTE EXCAVATION
A Greek from one city was, by definition, not a citizen of another. Thus a Corinthian living in Athens could not – as a 'metic', or resident alien – own land, give his daughters in marriage to an Athenian or take part in some religious ceremonies, and had to pay a special tax. Greek cities very rarely extended citizenship to others – an important difference from the Romans, who gradually extended citizen-rights amongst the peoples they conquered.

RELATED HISTORIES
THE *POLIS*
page 16

POLITICS & DEMOCRACY
page 38

ASPASIA
page 44

SLAVERY
page 48

3-SECOND BIOGRAPHIES
SOLON
born ca. 640 BCE
Athenian 'lawgiver', who grouped the citizens of Athens into property classes and gave even the poorest some political rights

CLEISTHENES
born ca. 565 BCE
Athenian politician, often regarded as the founder of democracy

30-SECOND TEXT
Timothy Duff

Only (male) citizens could participate fully in the life of a Greek city-state.

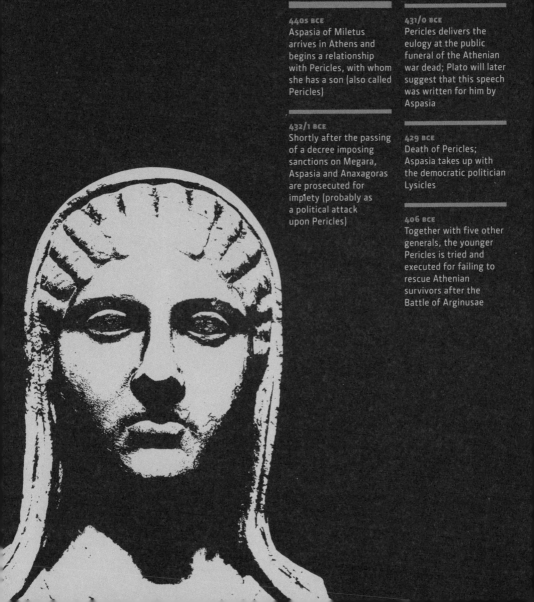

440S BCE
Aspasia of Miletus arrives in Athens and begins a relationship with Pericles, with whom she has a son (also called Pericles)

432/1 BCE
Shortly after the passing of a decree imposing sanctions on Megara, Aspasia and Anaxagoras are prosecuted for impiety (probably as a political attack upon Pericles)

431/0 BCE
Pericles delivers the eulogy at the public funeral of the Athenian war dead; Plato will later suggest that this speech was written for him by Aspasia

429 BCE
Death of Pericles; Aspasia takes up with the democratic politician Lysicles

406 BCE
Together with five other generals, the younger Pericles is tried and executed for failing to rescue Athenian survivors after the Battle of Arginusae

ASPASIA

As the mistress of the leading statesman Pericles from the 440s until his death in 429 BCE, Aspasia of Miletus was one of the most notorious women in fifth-century Athens, and was perhaps the most politically influential. According to the ancient biographer Plutarch, Pericles was so devoted to her that he set aside his legitimate wife in her favour. Since Aspasia was not Athenian, their children would not qualify for Athenian citizenship. Plutarch records that Pericles asked for, and was granted, a special exception to this rule for his son by Aspasia after all his legitimate children died of plague.

Ancient sources describe Aspasia as 'infamous' and 'clever with words', attributing much of her attraction for Pericles and other leading men to her persuasive skills. In his dialogue *Menexenus*, Plato has Socrates claim that Aspasia taught Pericles rhetoric and that she composed some of his most important speeches, including the famous Funeral Oration. The comic poet Aristophanes goes even further: in his *Acharnians* (produced in 425 BCE), the hero Dicaeopolis alleges that a principal cause of the Peloponnesian War was Pericles' anger at another city's abduction of prostitutes from a brothel Aspasia was running. These stories should be treated with scepticism, and Dicaeopolis's claim is clearly meant as a parody of the series of abductions of women with which Herodotus opens his *Histories*. Together with other attacks by comic poets, they nevertheless give an idea of the suspicion in which Aspasia was held. Talk of her intellect and rhetorical fluency links her with Sophists in Athens such as Anaxagoras, who was said to have taught Pericles philosophy and with whom she may have been prosecuted for impiety in the late 430s. Certainly her career seems to embody the opposite of Pericles' own prescription to Athenian women: 'to be heard of as little as possible among men, whether for virtue or blame'.

Although details of her life are scant, Aspasia is also interesting to social historians as the most famous example of a *hetaira* ('companion', plural *hetairai*). These were educated and accomplished women who engaged in long-term affairs with leading citizens. Such relationships involved exchanging sexual favours for financial security, and *hetairai* came from the ranks of women (resident aliens, freed slaves) unqualified for citizen marriage. It has been suggested that *hetairai*, who were often more worldly and educated than Athenian women, may have offered a form of companionship citizen marriages lacked.

Katherine Harloe

HOME & FAMILY LIFE

the 30-second history

3-SECOND SURVEY
The household, or family, was the vital basic unit of Greek *polis* life.

3-MINUTE EXCAVATION
Xenophon suggests that while a dutiful wife was expected to remain secluded at home, it would be discreditable for the head of a wealthy household to do the same. He was expected to play a part in public life; this would include hosting visitors and fellow citizens at home. The drinking party or symposium became an important part of both *polis* and home life, but took place in 'men's quarters' rigorously kept separate from the women's part of the house.

Families were an important part of the *polis*, producing new generations of citizens from legitimate marriages. The Greek *oikos* or *oikia* can refer to a household as a social unit, but also as an economic entity: ideally, a rural household would consist of a farmer with his wife, children and slaves, working the farm; in town, a similar set of norms applied, though we might imagine that real life did not always match the ideal. The father was head of this family and represented it in the political and economic world beyond the house. His wife, led at marriage from her father's household to her groom's, was nominally confined to the domestic sphere and responsible for its smooth and productive running. Xenophon's *Oeconomicus* ('household matters', whence our word 'economics') gives one picture of how an Athenian gentleman farmer might instruct his young wife as his 'partner in their common estate'. She would manage their slaves and the products of their land, making wool into clothes, rearing children and caring for the sick. Sons stayed under the authority of their fathers until they were old enough to establish an *oikos* of their own; daughters stayed until their marriage. Children were expected to look after their parents in old age and arrange their funerals, as one generation gave way to the next.

RELATED HISTORIES
See also
CITIZENS
page 42

ASPASIA
page 44

SLAVERY
page 48

HOUSES & PALACES
page 128

3-SECOND BIOGRAPHIES
ISCOMACHUS
fifth century BCE
Well-born landowner, a character in Xenophon's *Oeconomicus* whose instructions to his young wife offer one model of Athenian marriage and family life

ANTIPHON
late fifth century BCE
Forensic orator whose courtroom speeches give us an insight into the workings of the Greek home

30-SECOND TEXT
Matthew Nicholls

Respectable family life and the symposium could both be part of the Greek home.

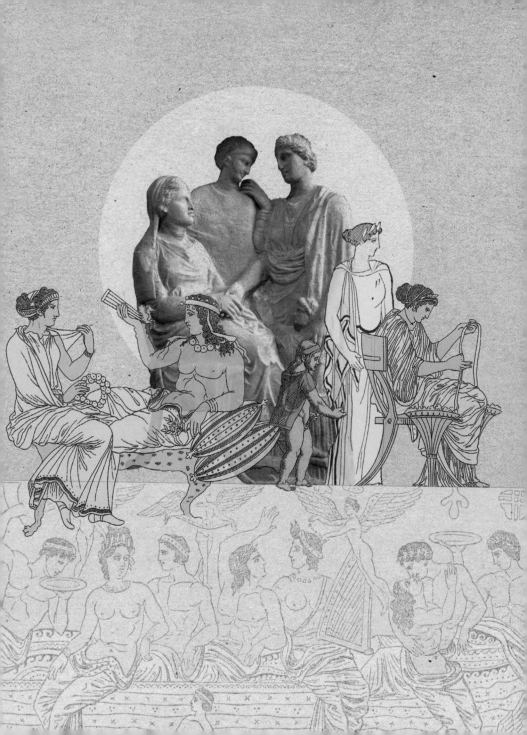

SLAVERY

the 30-second history

Slavery was widespread in

the ancient world, in Greece as elsewhere; the distinction between free and enslaved people was one of the great polarities of society. However, slavery can be hard to study because ancient writers did not consider it worth discussing in detail and slaves themselves left no literary and relatively little archaeological trace. Practices varied from place to place: Athens seems to have had a particularly large number of individually owned chattel slaves who could be bought and sold, while Sparta relied on a huge permanent population of serf-like 'helots'. The sheer number of slaves (around a third of the population of Attica, for example) meant that they were an integral part of the economy of the Greek world. From the thousands of slaves toiling in the Athenian silver mines at Laurium to agricultural, industrial and domestic work, the labour of slaves enabled some of the greatest achievements of the Greeks. A fortunate few were treated generously and valued for their skills, earning affection, the chance of some sort of family life, and eventually freedom; life for the majority was much less privileged. Slaves were legally protected but as property, not as human beings, and had little recourse against ill treatment.

RELATED HISTORIES
See also
CITIZENS
page 42

AGRICULTURE
page 50

TRADE & THE ECONOMY
page 52

3-SECOND BIOGRAPHY
AESOP
ca.seventh–sixth century BCE
Supposed author of popular fables; unreliable biographical sources claim that he started life as a slave

30-SECOND TEXT
Matthew Nicholls

3-SECOND SURVEY
Slavery was a universal feature of the ancient Greek world, seen as a natural element of human society.

3-MINUTE EXCAVATION
Slaves – mostly non-Greeks – could be kidnapped, captured in war, punished for crimes or debt by enslavement, or even sold by desperate parents. Slavery was apparently accepted as the natural order of things: even the great philosophers offer little systematic ethical enquiry into it. Enslavement seems to have been regarded either as bad luck or the consequence of natural inferiority – either way, the privileged (and free) Greeks who wrote our literary sources saw little reason to question it.

Slaves performed a wide variety of jobs in the Greek world, underpinning its economy.

AGRICULTURE

the 30-second history

3-SECOND SURVEY
Much of Greek farming
was a matter of survival
in the face of an often
uncooperative landscape,
and farming strategies were
geared towards efficiency
and risk-management.

3-MINUTE EXCAVATION
Unlike the Romans, the
Greeks have not left us
detailed technical treatises
on farming. For them,
agriculture was a matter
of following longstanding
tradition, and since it was
so widespread no one
required a manual! The
authors who do deal with
farming – Hesiod in the
seventh century BCE,
Xenophon in the fifth and
fourth – dwell more on its
virtue than its methods: the
good farmer was the good
citizen, in Greek eyes, unlike
shiftless wandering
merchants.

Farming was not a niche activity
in ancient Greece: a large proportion of Greeks
owned and worked land, or – if rich enough –
had slaves to do it for them. For poorer citizens,
farming was on the level of subsistence;
producing just enough to feed their families,
they were at the mercy of a run of bad harvests.
Understanding Greek farming means understanding
the Greek landscape. The typical city-state
comprised a limited area of cultivable land,
bounded by mountains on whose peaks crops
would not grow, though sheep and goats could
graze upon their sparse vegetation. Low rainfall
limited the production of cereals, especially
wheat; barley can survive in drier conditions,
so barley bread and porridge were the staple of
the poor Greek's diet, with wheat a luxury. Meat
too was for special occasions, such as religious
festivals, since eating animals is an inefficient use
of their calorific potential: better to keep them
alive and extract from them milk, wool and (in the
case of draught-oxen) labour. Farmers typically
grew a range of arable crops (cereals, legumes,
vines and trees) rather than specializing – this
lessened the risk of catastrophic crop-failure
in case of blight, drought or enemy invasion.
Greece's agricultural product *par excellence* was
the olive, considered emblematic of the hardy and
resilient people who cultivated it.

RELATED HISTORIES
See also
CITIZENS
page 42

HOME & FAMILY LIFE
page 46

SLAVERY
page 48

TRADE & THE ECONOMY
page 52

3-SECOND BIOGRAPHIES
HESIOD
fl. ca. 700 BCE
Epic poet who sang of farming
and the passage of seasons

THEOPHRASTUS
ca. 371–287 BCE
Philosopher, the first to treat
plants and their cultivation to
systematic study

XENOPHON
born ca. 430 BCE
Wrote the dialogue
Oeconomicus, or Economics

30-SECOND TEXT
Emma Aston

*The rhythms of the
agricultural year were
central to Greek life.*

TRADE & THE ECONOMY

the 30-second history

The Linear B tablets of Bronze

Age Crete show that sea-borne long-distance trade was carried on between the Mycenaeans and other peoples before their civilization collapsed around 1200 BCE. As the Greek world began to emerge from the dark centuries that followed, a renewal of trade was one sign of new growth. Our early literary sources, written for and sometimes by an aristocratic land-owning elite, tend to look down on professional traders. It was trading ships, however, that brought new goods and ideas (such as the Phoenician alphabet) into the Greek world, and allowed Greek states to grow by buying and selling each other's surplus agricultural or industrial products. Grain, oil and wine were joined by pottery, metals, slaves, textiles and luxury goods on merchant ships plying the Aegean and Mediterranean seas in the summer sailing season. Over time trading ports (*emporia*) grew up as centres of trade between Greek states and with non-Greek economies in Egypt and Italy. Athens' pre-eminence in the fifth century BCE, and her maritime empire that helped keep the sea free of pirates, saw her port of Piraeus turn into one of the Greek world's largest trading places, though much of her trade was carried out by non-citizen 'resident aliens' called metics.

3-SECOND SURVEY
Trade was an important pillar of the Greek world's economy, though less socially prestigious than agriculture or warfare.

3-MINUTE EXCAVATION
Land transport was expensive in mountainous Greece, but sea transport, though not cheap, allowed a lively trading economy to develop. Athenian orator Isocrates praised Athens' port of Piraeus as 'a market of such abundance that articles which it is difficult to obtain from the rest of the world, one here, one there, are easy to obtain at Athens'.

RELATED HISTORIES
See also
'FROGS AROUND A POND'
page 24

CITIZENS
page 42

AGRICULTURE
page 50

LINEAR B & THE ALPHABET
page 100

3-SECOND BIOGRAPHIES
SOSTRATUS
fl. late sixth century BCE
Greek merchant from Aegina who traded across the Mediterranean; known from an inscribed stone anchor that he dedicated to Apollo at Gravisca in Etruria, Italy

ISOCRATES
436–338 BCE
Athenian orator whose speeches offer valuable insight into Greek life

30-SECOND TEXT
Matthew Nicholls

Trade (especially by sea) helped spread ideas, goods and people around the Greek world and beyond.

MYTH & RELIGION

city-state See *polis*

cult The practice of religious sacrifice, ceremony and worship offered to a divine or semi-divine figure.

Elysian Fields The blissful portion of the Underworld reserved for the souls of heroes and the especially deserving dead.

epic verse Long poems narrating the deeds of heroes; composed in rolling 'dactylic hexameter', probably originally as an oral form of poetry, by bards like Homer.

Hades The Greek god of the Underworld, and also the name of his underground realm of the dead.

Linear B Syllabic writing system used to record an early form of Greek, around 1450–1200 BCE. Preserved chiefly on clay tablets excavated in Crete and other Mycenaean sites, which mostly record lists of commodities.

mantic Relating to prophecy and divination (from the Greek '*mantis*', a prophet or seer).

Mount Olympus The tallest mountain in Greece, often thought of as the home of the twelve Olympian gods, and particularly Zeus.

***polis* (plural *poleis*)** The *polis*, or city-state (with surrounding territory), was the essential political unit of the ancient Greek world, with its own citizen body and legislative structures.

sanctuary An enclosure set aside for religious purposes, sacred to a particular god or gods. Contained an altar for sacrifice and sometimes temples or other structures for visitors and officials, including (at some sites) provision for healing, for athletic games or for other activities associated with the sanctuary's deity.

Titan A race of divine giants of enormous strength, overthrown by the Olympian gods.

tyrant A Greek term for an autocratic king-like ruler; not necessarily pejorative.

Underworld The realm of the dead. See Hades

Vedic Relating to the Indian Vedas, the oldest scriptures of Hinduism, composed in Sanskrit in the second millennium BCE.

GODS

the 30-second history

According to the historian

Herodotus, worshipping the same gods (along with shared blood, language and customs) was one of the things that marked Greeks out as Greeks. The most important gods had many different cults and temples; the greatest festivals, such as those of Zeus at Olympia or Dionysus at Athens, attracted worshippers from across the Greek world. But despite the centrality of the gods to Greek life, there was no central religious authority or priestly caste, no holy book whose account of the gods was beyond criticism. Oracles, most famously Apollo's at Delphi, claimed to convey the responses of a god to mortal inquiry, but these could be obscurely misleading; false oracles were put down to the corruption of the god's intermediaries. The gods were imagined as being concerned with their own worship and prerogatives, but also with human morality more generally; philosophers debated the question of whether such morality had an independent existence or was dependent on divine sanction. Atheism was rare, but not unheard of; for instance, a speaker in Critias' play *Sisyphus* (late fifth century BCE) argued that the gods were the invention of a shrewd man who wanted to eliminate wrongdoing by instilling in humanity the fear of divine overseers.

3-SECOND SURVEY
In a diverse world of competing city-states, worshipping the same gods was a key unifying feature of Greek identity.

3-MINUTE EXCAVATION
The idea of the Twelve Olympian gods was familiar at least as early as the sixth century BCE, when Pisistratus, tyrant of Athens, set up an altar to 'the twelve gods'. But it is typical of the lack of any central religious authority that there was no set list of which gods were included: sometimes Heracles featured, for example, sometimes not. Compare the slight differences in the lists of the twelve apostles found in the Christian gospels.

RELATED HISTORIES
See also
HEROES & DEMIGODS
page 60

MYTH
page 62

ZEUS
page 64

ORACLES
page 68

SACRED ARCHITECTURE
page 122

3-SECOND BIOGRAPHIES
PISISTRATUS
died 527 BCE
Tyrant of Athens

HERODOTUS
ca. 485–ca. 424 BCE
Father (first writer) of history

CRITIAS
ca. 460–403 BCE
Politician and poet

30-SECOND TEXT
Patrick Finglass

The Greeks believed in variety of gods, each had particular interest and responsibilities.

HEROES & DEMIGODS

the 30-second history

The Greek word *heros*, from which our word 'hero' derives, is used by Homer to describe the mighty warriors of the Trojan War. These heroes, the leading fighters of the Greeks and Trojans, often had a divine parent, such as Achilles' mother Thetis or Sarpedon's father Zeus, yet they themselves were emphatically mortal. In the *Iliad* even the mighty Heracles is said to have died – something that reflects the tragic character of that poem, which places such an emphasis on the unbridgeable gap between human and divine. Elsewhere in Greek culture, by contrast, the gods' children and other figures of myth were believed to retain supernatural power after death. Some, like Heracles or the Dioscuri (Castor and Polydeuces), were worshipped as gods throughout the Greek world; more commonly, a hero or heroine had one prominent cult where s/he was believed to be buried. Real people, not just the figures of myth, could also be recognized as heroes: soldiers killed in war, founders of new settlements and successful athletes could all have prayers and sacrifices offered to them after their deaths. At the end of the fifth century BCE the Spartan admiral Lysander received cultic honours when alive, presaging a custom that was developed further in the Hellenistic period, and by the Romans, especially in the case of their emperors.

3-SECOND SURVEY
The Greeks believed that the spirits of certain powerful deceased individuals had the power to help and harm them in their daily lives.

3-MINUTE EXCAVATION
'Hero' in English denotes a brave and admirable person, but the recipients of the Greek hero cult were often anything but. In 492 BCE an unsuccessful boxer, Cleomedes of Astypalaea, in his anger destroyed a school full of children, and hid in a chest in the sanctuary of Athena, which when opened was found to be empty; the Delphic oracle then instructed the Astypalaeans to honour Cleomedes with sacrifices 'as the last of the heroes'.

RELATED HISTORIES
See also
GODS
page 58

MYTH
page 62

3-SECOND BIOGRAPHIES
LYSANDER
died 395 BCE
Successful Spartan admiral in the Peloponnesian War

AUGUSTUS
63 BCE–14 CE
First Roman emperor, widely worshipped during and after his lifetime by inhabitants of the Roman empire, including Greeks

30-SECOND TEXT
Patrick Finglass

The heroic figures of epic poetry and myth, and even some historical figures, could be thought of or worshipped as god-like.

MYTH

the 30-second history

Greek literature and art are

dominated by myth: the deeds of gods and heroes, covering a period of time from the creation of the universe to the Trojan War and its aftermath. There was no 'authorized version' of the Greek myths; no one had the authority to impose their account as the only true one, and individual writers, artists and communities adapted myths to suit their purposes, both literary and political. So Pindar calls Heracles 'short of stature' in a poem praising a ruler who was probably himself vertically challenged; and the Spartans assert their right to command the Greek forces against Persia because their former king, Agamemnon, had held that privilege at Troy. Myth provided not only a marvellously flexible core subject-matter for poetry, but also a foundation for prose; the difference between myth and history took time to become firmly established, and historians such as Herodotus, and even Thucydides (who claims that his *History* lacks a mythological element), frequently look to myth for antecedents and explanations of events in their own time. Great surveys of myth were compiled later in antiquity by writers such as Apollodorus, the forerunners of modern collections. Greek myth had a powerful impact on the stories told by the Romans, and still inspires art and literature today.

3-SECOND SURVEY
Greek myths enjoyed long-lasting popularity not just because they were exciting stories, but also because they encouraged those who heard and read them to reflect on the human condition.

3-MINUTE EXCAVATION
The differences between accounts of a particular myth could be surprisingly significant. So in early versions of the Medea myth, Medea's children were killed by her enemies in Corinth, or by Medea herself by mistake; but in his play of 431 BCE Euripides radically altered the myth's impact by making Medea deliberately murder her children to punish her former husband. Familiar today, this version must have appeared strikingly original when first performed.

RELATED HISTORIES
See also
GODS
page 58

HEROES & DEMIGODS
page 60

HOMER & EPIC POETRY
page 78

HISTORY: HERODOTUS
& THUCYDIDES
page 86

3-SECOND BIOGRAPHIES
PINDAR
ca. 522–ca. 443 BCE
Writer of lyric poetry in honour of victorious athletes and wealthy patrons

EURIPIDES
ca. 480s–406 BCE
Athenian tragic playwright

30-SECOND TEXT
Patrick Finglass

Myths were powerful, flexible stories about the deeds of gods and heroes, told as folktales and used by poets such as Pindar.

ZEUS

Zeus, god of the sky, was king of the Greek gods, mightier than all the others put together. His father, the Titan Cronus (or Kronos), had been told that one of his children would succeed him, and as a result swallowed them all as they were born; but Cronus' wife Rhea substituted a stone in place of Zeus, whom she spirited away to a cave in Crete. When he grew up, he overcame his father, consigning him and his fellow Titans to the Underworld, and freed his brothers and sisters.

By his wife, Hera, Zeus fathered Hephaestus and Ares; but he was far from monogamous, and had children by other goddesses (Athena by Maia, Apollo and Artemis by Leto) and by mortal women (Heracles by Alcmena, Perseus by Danaë, and so on). This impressive progeny may result from Zeus's identification with a series of other, now forgotten, heroes and divinities. Zeus's own name is very old indeed, occurring on the Linear B tablets. The god 'Dyaus Pita' who appears in Vedic texts of the second millennium BCE has a name that corresponds exactly to the Greek 'Zeus Pater' or 'Father Zeus', indicating an origin among the Indo-Europeans, the ancestors of both peoples.

Zeus plays a major part in works of Greek literature: Homer's *Iliad* announces that 'the plan of Zeus was being brought to pass', but the exact nature of and motivations for that plan remain mysterious. By convention, Zeus never appeared on the tragic stage, but his purposes were thought to stand behind the actions – the final words of Sophocles' *Trachiniae*, after the audience have seen Zeus's own son Heracles wracked by agonizing pains, are 'there is none of these things that is not Zeus', inviting the audience to consider why Zeus might have allowed his son to undergo such appalling suffering. The statue of Zeus of Olympia carved by the Athenian sculptor Phidias became one of the Seven Wonders of the World, and was thought to have been inspired by verses from Homer describing how the shaking of Zeus's head made Mount Olympus tremble. Temples to Zeus were erected all over the Greek world, of which Olympia was perhaps the most famous; the games there were held in his honour. The Romans identified him with Jupiter, another god of the sky whose name derived from the same Indo-European source.

Patrick Finglass

CEREMONY & SACRIFICE

the 30-second history

Ancient Greek lives were

circumscribed by rituals, symbolic acts designed to maintain a harmonious relationship with the gods. These took place within the home, at the level of the *polis*, and at interregional sanctuaries like Delphi; they included processions, hymns and various offerings of objects, food and drink. However, arguably the central ceremony in Greek religion was animal sacrifice, in which a carefully chosen victim was killed for a specific deity or deities. Typically the animal was killed at the altar, stunned by a blow from an axe and its throat slit before the meat was divided into symbolic portions for consumption by gods and humans. To us, sacrifice contains a basic puzzle: if the gods are immortal, why do they need meat? There seem to have been two answers. First, though deathless, the gods enjoyed the savoury smoke of the carcass, which rose up to heaven when burned at the conclusion of the rite. Second, sacrifice conferred honour, *timê*, which gods craved as much as mortals. The greatest honour came from large and expensive victims – bovines especially – whose slaughter was a major economic loss to a community or individual: a sacrifice in every sense of the word.

RELATED HISTORIES
See also
AGRICULTURE
page 50

GODS
page 58

HEROES & DEMIGODS
page 60

PANHELLENIC FESTIVALS
page 70

SACRED ARCHITECTURE
page 122

3-SECOND BIOGRAPHY
MENANDER
ca. 342–292 BCE
Athenian comic playwright whose surviving plays tell us a lot about ancient customs, beliefs and attitudes

30-SECOND TEXT
Emma Aston

3-SECOND SURVEY
How can gods and humans maintain a social contract? For the Greeks, the key way was sacrifice, in which prized livestock was ceremonially slaughtered to give the gods the honour they demanded.

3-MINUTE EXCAVATION
Sacrifice kept gods happy, but it had tangible benefits for humans too. It provided a rare chance to eat meat in communities whose workaday diets were, of necessity, largely vegetarian. Ancient playwright Menander comments on this bitterly in his comedy *The Peevish Man*, describing how people turn up to a sacrifice with picnic-boxes and jugs of wine and eat all the best cuts of meat while the god gets the tailbone and gallbladder.

Sacrifices tried to win the favour of the gods with offerings including animals great and small.

ORACLES

the 30-second history

3-SECOND SURVEY
In a world governed by supernatural forces, oracles provided a glimpse of divine will and helped mortals plan their lives and solve their crises.

3-MINUTE EXCAVATION
Divination (the process of learning the future, or the hidden present) could be done at home on a small scale, for those unable or unwilling to travel to an oracular sanctuary. 'DIY' techniques included cleromancy (drawing lots), oneiromancy (interpreting dreams) and the decipherment of various natural signs such as the flight of birds or even sudden human sneezes. For the ancient Greeks, the world was full of messages and symbols, waiting to be read.

We think of the world around us as largely susceptible to rational explanation, but this was not so for the ancient Greeks. Warfare and weather, health and childbirth – such life-changing matters were directed by supernatural forces whose workings were obscure. Faced by such uncertainty, both states and individuals consulted oracular sanctuaries, holy sites where a particular god would give pronouncements if suitably approached. Famous oracular sanctuaries included that of Apollo at Delphi, that of Zeus at Dodona and that of Trophonius at Lebadea. Different procedures were followed at every site. At Delphi, the Pythia (Apollo's priestess) is said to have delivered the oracles while under the influence of fumes rising from a chasm in the rock. At Dodona, rustling oak leaves, clanging cauldrons and the cooing of sacred doves were apparently involved, though precisely how is uncertain. Lebadea is perhaps the most peculiar case: according to the second-century CE travel writer Pausanias, those wishing to consult Trophonius were whisked into an underground chamber by unseen forces, and experienced mantic revelations that left them temporarily unable to laugh. In all cases, human visitors were allowed brief access – valuable, but disquieting – to a world beyond their own.

RELATED HISTORIES
See also
GODS
page 58

HEROES & DEMIGODS
page 60

ZEUS
page 64

CEREMONY & SACRIFICE
page 66

PANHELLENIC FESTIVALS
page 70

SACRED ARCHITECTURE
page 122

3-SECOND BIOGRAPHY
PYTHIA
eighth century BCE–393 CE
Title of the female mouthpiece of the god Apollo at Delphi, who pronounced oracles while wearing a laurel crown

30-SECOND TEXT
Emma Aston

Greeks tried to see clues from the gods in oracles such as Delphi's Pythia, or natural signs like the flight of birds.

PANHELLENIC FESTIVALS

the 30-second history

All ancient communities held
religious festivals in honour of specific deities, occasions for conviviality and the reinforcement of collective traditions. However, a few festivals in major religious sanctuaries enjoyed 'Panhellenic status', attracting attendance from all over the Greek world and beyond. These festivals involved competitions in athletics (including foot-races, boxing and wrestling), horse-racing, drama, music or a combination of these events, and the most prestigious were the so-called 'Crown Games': the Olympian and the Nemean in the Peloponnese, the Isthmian near Corinth and the Pythian at Delphi. These festivals are best understood by asking what participants got out of them. To take the example of someone running in the *stadion* (sprint) at Olympia: he would be able to display his speed and strength, the excellence of his training, the development of his physique (something well-born Greeks took seriously), his noble lineage and, last but not least, his piety towards the presiding god, in this case Zeus. His home state would share in the glory if he won, and his victory might be immortalized in an ode by a famous poet such as Pindar, ensuring lasting renown. Finally, while at the Games he would meet up with his rich friends and share the latest news from across the Greek world.

3-SECOND SURVEY
Panhellenic festivals brought Greeks together from their various regions and city-states in a celebration of shared values and religious observance.

3-MINUTE EXCAVATION
The importance of the Panhellenic festivals as expressions of Hellenic unity can only be appreciated when one realizes how disunited the Greeks actually were in political terms. Greece did not formally become a nation until the nineteenth century CE; in antiquity it comprised many separate city-states, frequently at war with one another. The sacred truces imposed during the Crown Games allowed participants to travel and compete in a rare condition of safety and harmony.

RELATED HISTORIES
See also
THE *POLIS*
page 16

GREEKS & BARBARIANS
page 36

CEREMONY & SACRIFICE
page 66

SACRED ARCHITECTURE
page 122

ENTERTAINMENT
ARCHITECTURE
page 132

30-SECOND TEXT
Emma Aston

The Panhellenic games, spanning the Greek world, are a forerunner of today's truly global Olympic games.

AFTERLIFE

the 30-second history

3-SECOND SURVEY
Death, for the Greeks, was not the end: belief in an afterlife was almost universal, and it was held that contact with the dead was possible through certain ritual methods.

3-MINUTE EXCAVATION
Where was the Underworld? Various places in the Greek world claimed to possess its entrance, generally a cave or significant hole in the ground. One of the most famous was at Taenarum, in the Peloponnese: Heracles was said to have dragged the hell-hound Cerberus up through this portal as one of his Labours. But the travel writer Pausanias (second century CE) peered into the recesses of the cave and was disappointed to find no channel leading down into Hades.

Unlike the Judaeo-Christian tradition of Heaven and Hell, Greek afterlife beliefs did not, initially, contain the element of moral judgement. In early epic verse, the important dead – semi-divine heroes who fell in glorious battle – had the possibility of a privileged afterlife (in the Elysian Fields or similar imagined location), while ordinary people endured the obscurity of Hades, but the distinction was not made on grounds of virtue. An ethical dimension had, however, begun to creep in by the fourth century BCE: Plato's *Phaedo* describes good souls attaining repose while those of villains wander in bewilderment through the Underworld. The Greeks believed that the dead had special powers and knowledge, which could be harnessed with the correct rituals. In Homer's *Odyssey*, Odysseus voyages to the land of the dead to consult the seer Tiresias, but such supernatural journeys were not possible for normal people: instead, they might travel to a *nekyomanteion*, or oracle of the dead, to communicate with a deceased relation or acquaintance. Different *nekyomanteia* worked differently, but a common theme was some kind of descent underground, into a dark and forbidding space, to achieve proximity and contact with the shades. Offerings were also required: the dead could be destructive and vengeful if not properly placated.

RELATED HISTORIES
See also
MYTH
page 62

CEREMONY & SACRIFICE
page 66

ORACLES
page 68

PANHELLENIC FESTIVALS
page 70

SACRED ARCHITECTURE
page 122

3-SECOND BIOGRAPHY
PAUSANIAS
ca. 125–180 CE
Travel writer who provides us with our most detailed surviving description of ancient sites, customs and myths

30-SECOND TEXT
Emma Aston

Greeks had differing ideas about the afterlife, but the paradise of the Elysian Fields and the gloom of Hades were commonly shared beliefs.

LITERATURE

barbarian A Greek term for a non-Greek, defined in opposition to traditional Greek characteristics and behaviours. Unable to speak and reason in Greek (hence, making an inarticulate 'bar-bar' sound), or exercise moral judgement and self-control.

chorus A group of performers who spoke, sang and danced as an extra 'character' in a Greek play, offering commentary and advice on the unfolding action.

city-state See *polis*

Dionysia Athenian festival in honour of Dionysus, god of wine and drama. Held in March, the festival rites included competitive performances of tragic and comic plays, as well as sacrifices, a procession of war orphans and other religious and civic elements.

epic poem Long poem narrating the deeds of heroes; composed in rolling 'dactylic hexameter', probably originally as an oral form of poetry, by bards like Homer.

Lenaea Another Athenian festival in honour of Dionysus, god of wine and drama. Held in January/February, the festival rites included dramatic contests in tragedy and comedy from the second half of the fifth century BCE.

lyric poem One of the three chief Greek verse forms (from the seventh century BCE onwards), along with drama and epic. Lyric poetry was composed to be sung, often to the lyre. Choral lyrics included songs in praise of gods, rulers or athletes, while 'monodic' or solo lyric poems often treated more personal themes such as love.

metre The pattern or rhythm of ancient Greek poetry. The basic element of Greek metre was syllable length, long or short; combinations of longs and shorts made patterns considered characteristic of different verse forms.

polis (plural poleis) The *polis*, or city-state (with surrounding territory), was the essential political unit of the ancient Greek world, with its own citizen body and legislative structures.

rhetoric The art of public speaking. An important skill for the Greek statesman, and an important part of Greek elite education, because the art of persuasion through speech-making was crucial in many spheres of political and judicial activity.

satyr Mythical companion of the god Dionysus, combining human and animal characteristics; associated, like Dionysus, both with self-indulgence and with culture.

symposium Drinking party for Greek men, held in the home, with entertainment ranging from drinking games and flute girls to philosophical discussions.

telos In Aristotelian philosophical thought, the purpose or end for which an object exists.

HOMER & EPIC POETRY

the 30-second history

Homer was the name the Greeks

gave to a legendary and uniquely gifted poet, who had sung of the glorious deeds of gods and heroes in the distant past. His most famous works are the *Iliad*, which tells the story of Achilles, the greatest Greek warrior of the Trojan War; and the *Odyssey*, which tells of another Greek hero Odysseus's long and arduous journey home to his faithful wife Penelope from the exotic fringes of the world. Most scholars today doubt that a single individual composed these works, thinking instead that they stem from a centuries-long tradition of oral poetry. How and when they were first written down is a matter of considerable debate. Fifth-century Greeks attributed many other poems to Homer besides the *Iliad* and *Odyssey*. These include the 'Little Iliad', which tells the story of the fall of Troy by the trick of the wooden horse, and the comedic 'Battle of Frogs and Mice'. Homer was therefore seen as the father of all literary genres, comic and tragic; and the *Iliad* and *Odyssey* have been called the 'Bible' of the Greeks. Together with that of Hesiod, another early and possibly non-existent epic poet, Homer's poetry provides the foundation of Greek literary culture.

RELATED HISTORIES
See also
GODS
page 58

HEROES & DEMIGODS
page 60

MYTH
page 62

PANHELLENIC FESTIVALS
page 70

3-SECOND SURVEY
Many scholars today think Homer never existed as an individual, but was a fiction invented by later Greeks.

3-MINUTE EXCAVATION
If Homer's epics were not originally written down, how were they preserved and disseminated? This question has exercised scholars for two centuries. Rather than memorization, most favour the notion of composition-in-performance, where a highly skilled singer would recombine traditional phrases, scenes and larger narrative blocks from a common stock passed down through generations. Comparative studies of living epic traditions, such as those of the former Yugoslavia, lend weight to this hypothesis.

3-SECOND BIOGRAPHIES
HOMER
active second half of eighth century BCE if he existed
Legendary poet of the Trojan War

HESIOD
fl. ca. 700 BCE
Epic poet who sang of the gods, of farming and the passage of the seasons

30-SECOND TEXT
Katherine Harloe

Epic poems told of the mighty deeds of great heroes like the wily Odysseus, or warriors like Hector and Achilles.

TRAGEDY

the 30-second history

Tragedy is one of the most

successful Greek inventions: it gave rise to a tradition of world literature which links names such as Shakespeare, Goethe and Soyinka; inspired opera and other genres; informed a philosophical outlook; and is invoked daily to characterize terrible events. Our view of Greek tragedy has a particularly Athenian flavour, as almost all surviving examples were produced in Athens at festivals of Dionysus, the god of wine and disguise. The Athenian audience's stamina was considerable. On each day of tragic shows they would sit through three tragedies, followed by a less serious satyr drama. The festival was not mere entertainment, but an important religious and civic occasion. Aeschylus, Sophocles and Euripides are the most famous tragedians, but they composed only a small subset of the hundreds staged in the fifth century BCE. Tragedies consist of choral songs alternating with individual speeches or dialogue, with chorus and dialogue differing in dialect and metre. They portray the fates of heroes from mythical times, such as the Trojan Wars, although one surviving example (Aeschylus's *Persians*) concerns historical events. Aristotle claimed that tragedy developed out of choruses in honour of Dionysus. Some scholars believe instead that it was an Athenian invention of the late sixth or early fifth century BCE.

3-SECOND SURVEY
Tragedies – plays performed in honour of the god Dionysus – were a central part of ancient Athenian cultural life.

3-MINUTE EXCAVATION
Satyr drama is tragedy's less well known little sister. Only Euripides' *Cyclops* survives complete; although fragments amounting to around half of Sophocles' *Trackers* were discovered in Egypt in the early 1900s. Satyr dramas are distinguished by their choruses of satyrs: half-men, half-goats, whose desires for wine and sex are often used to comic effect. Satyrs are also traditional followers of the god Dionysus. Their presence onstage may relate to tragedy's ritual origins.

RELATED HISTORIES
See also
HEROES & DEMIGODS
page 60

MYTH
page 62

PANHELLENIC FESTIVALS
page 70

COMEDY
page 82

3-SECOND BIOGRAPHIES
AESCHYLUS
ca. 525–456 BCE
First of the triumvirate of fam Athenian tragic dramatists

SOPHOCLES
ca. 495–406 BCE
Athenian tragic dramatist, aut of *Oedipus the King*

EURIPIDES
ca. 480s–406 BCE
Athenian tragic dramatist, aut of *Medea* and *Bacchae*

30-SECOND TEXT
Katherine Harloe

Audiences enjoyed th tragic tales of heroes and gods, performed by masked actors.

COMEDY

the 30-second history

Alongside tragedy and satyr-play, comedy was one of three types of drama performed at Athens. Contests between comic playwrights took place at festivals in honour of Dionysus – at the Dionysia from 486 BCE, and at the Lenaea from 442 BCE. Eleven plays by Aristophanes survive, usually centred round a comic hero who achieves fantastical goals, such as flying to heaven on a dung beetle to bring back Peace to the weary Greeks (*Peace*, 421 BCE), or descending into Hades to recover the recently deceased Euripides to inspire the Athenians (*Frogs*, 405 BCE – a play named after its chorus, who sing to the hero as he crosses the river of the Underworld). Humour in such dramas could be deviously literary (learned parody of archaic poetry) or unashamedly scatological, sometimes both at the same time. These plays also mocked well-known figures of the day, including leading politicians, and very occasionally gave specific political advice, as when in *Frogs* Aristophanes urges the restoration of political rights to a group of disenfranchised citizens – advice which won him a crown of sacred olive from the Athenian state. Comedies from the Classical period were reperformed throughout antiquity, and had a decisive influence on the Roman playwrights Plautus and Terence, and, through them, on comic drama down to our own day.

3-SECOND SURVEY
Comic drama offered Athenian audiences a potent mix of spectacle, escapism and intensely topical political commentary.

3-MINUTE EXCAVATION
Greek comedy was divided by ancient scholars into three periods: Old Comedy (fifth century BCE), frequently centred on a comic hero, Middle Comedy (early fourth century BCE), associated with mythological satire, and New Comedy (late fourth century BCE), which eschewed myth for plots based on realistic human relationships. The chorus, so important in Old Comedy as key allies or adversaries of the protagonist, became progressively less prominent as the genre focused more and more on the actors.

RELATED HISTORIES
See also
PANHELLENIC FESTIVALS
page 70

TRAGEDY
page 80

3-SECOND BIOGRAPHIES
CRATINUS
ca. 519–422 BCE
Athenian comic playwright

ARISTOPHANES
ca. 450–386 BCE
Athenian comic playwright

EUPOLIS
ca. 446–411 BCE
Athenian comic playwright

MENANDER
ca. 342–292 BCE
Athenian playwright of 'New Comedy'

30-SECOND TEXT
Patrick Finglass

Greek comedy included rude jokes and costumes, political satire and choruses of 'animals' such as frogs and birds.

Late seventh century BCE
Sappho active on isle of Lesbos

ca. 600 BCE
Sappho reputed to have fled to exile in Sicily, accompanied by her daughter, Cleis

third century BCE
Nine books of Sappho's poetry, arranged according to metre, were collected in the library at Alexandria

60s/50s BCE
The Roman poet Catull adapts fragment 31 int Latin (his poem 51); adopts the pseudonym 'Lesbia' for the mistres addressed in his poetry collection

fourth–eleventh centuries CE
Surviving copies of Sappho's poetry allegedly burnt by the Christian Church

SAPPHO

Sappho is one of the only female voices to survive from ancient Greece, one of the most admired lyric poets in antiquity, and one of the most famous love poets of all time. Only a fraction of the nine books of her poetry collected in antiquity survives, and all but one poem are in fragments; but the corpus has been enriched over the past hundred years by new papyrus finds, including an almost complete poem first published in 2014. While most of Sappho's extant poetry is monody or 'personal' lyric, composed for solo performance in contexts such as the symposium, some fragments of choral songs survive.

The Roman poet Ovid immortalizes Sappho as the star-struck lover of the beautiful youth Phaon, passion for whom leads her to commit suicide by throwing herself from a cliff into the Ionian Sea. Yet her surviving lyrics celebrate women's beauty in erotic terms, and the term 'lesbian' derives from her homeland of Lesbos. One of her most famous songs, translated into Latin by the poet Catullus and quoted by the rhetorician Longinus in his treatise *On Sublimity*, describes the physical sensations that assail her on seeing her beloved accompanied by a man. This poem entered medical history as an account of the symptoms of erotic infatuation; in the twentieth century it attracted psychoanalytic interpretation as a depiction of Sappho's anxiety prompted by her homosexual 'perversion'.

More recently, feminist critics have moved away from reading Sappho's poetry as a mirror of her feelings and experiences, emphasizing instead how the homoerotic, feminine world she portrays provides a counterweight to the masculine ethos of much archaic Greek poetry. Fragment 16, for example, which excuses Helen's decision to leave her blameless husband Menelaus for the Trojan prince Paris, celebrates the irresistible force of desire as well as defending Homer's account of the Trojan War against alternative versions, such as that of the choral lyric poet Stesichorus, which relegated Helen to a lesser role. Poem 1 – the only one to have survived complete from antiquity – formally resembles the prayers for battlefield aid that Homeric heroes utter to the gods; here, though, Sappho calls Aphrodite to help her take revenge on a woman who spurns her love. Her sparse lyrics, musical language and arresting imagery have also attracted numerous modern translators, with Mary Barnard, Josephine Balmer and Anne Carson providing particularly accomplished versions.

Katherine Harloe

HISTORY: HERODOTUS & THUCYDIDES

the 30-second history

Cicero called Herodotus the 'father of history', yet until recently it was Thucydides who provided the model of history-writing as a truthful narrative of past political and military events. Both lived in the mid to late fifth century BCE; Herodotus hailed from Halicarnassus in Asia Minor and Thucydides from Athens. Herodotus wrote the history of the Persian Wars in nine books. It was he who first used the term '*historiē*' to characterize his work – although the Greek word is broad in meaning and best translated as 'inquiry'. His historical canvas is wide: as well as narrating the growth of the powers of Lydia and Persia, his work encompasses ethnographic descriptions of barbarian nations, accounts of local myths and traditions, even geographical speculations such as 'why does the Nile flood in summer?' These reflect the philosophical and scientific concerns of Ionian Greek thought of his time. Thucydides' account of the Peloponnesian War is narrower in focus, emphasizing diplomatic, political and military matters to the exclusion of other material. Thucydides and Herodotus are traditionally seen as offering opposed, even antagonistic models of history writing. Yet their works also display similarities: both are concerned with the rise of great political and military powers and with identifying the causes that led them into conflict.

3-SECOND SURVEY
Thucydides is seen as the father of political and military history, Herodotus of cultural history.

3-MINUTE EXCAVATION
What is history? Answers vary from a truthful account of past events, to an explanation of their causes, to any investigation that concerns singularities rather than generalizations. While Herodotus writes 'so that men's deeds will not fade over time', Thucydides designates his work a useful guide to the future, since 'the same or similar things will happen again'. This aligns it with social science, where it has been highly influential in politics and international relations.

RELATED HISTORIES
See also
PERSIAN & PELOPONNESIAN WARS
page 20

WARFARE
page 22

GREEKS & BARBARIANS
page 36

PHILOSOPHY: SOCRATES & PLATO
page 90

3-SECOND BIOGRAPHIES
HERODOTUS OF HALICARNASSUS
ca. 485–ca. 424 BCE
Historian of the Persian Wars

THUCYDIDES OF ATHENS
born ca. 460 BCE
Historian of, and military commander in, the Peloponnesian War

30-SECOND TEXT
Katherine Harloe

The historians Herodotus and Thucydides sought to explain the world and explored the reasons behind events.

ORATORY

the 30-second history

Already in the *Iliad* true heroism required a man to be both 'a speaker of words and a doer of deeds'; but not until the coming of the Greek city-state did the ability to persuade others in a civic context take on real importance, particularly in a democracy like Athens. In that city, any male citizen could address the assembly on matters of public policy, and bring a case before the law courts; matters of life and death would regularly be decided by the orator's skill. No presiding officer in either the assembly or the courts could rule material out of order; nothing stopped the able practitioner from stirring up his audience's passions to serve his cause. Unlike today, individuals spoke in the courts on their own behalf; this led to the growth of professional speech-writers, such as Isaeus and Lysias. The fifth century also saw the first formal study of rhetoric as an intellectual discipline, something first associated with the Syracusans Corax and Tisias, questioned by Plato in his *Gorgias*, and pursued by Aristotle in his *Rhetoric*. The rhetorical theory developed by the Greeks, as well as the speeches recorded by professional speech-writers and by historians, had a major impact on the development of rhetoric in the Roman world and beyond.

RELATED HISTORIES
See also
POLITICS & DEMOCRACY
page 38

LAW
page 40

3-SECOND SURVEY
Any Greek man looking for advancement within his city-state had to master the art of oratory.

3-MINUTE EXCAVATION
Oratory remained a profoundly ambiguous art: teachers of rhetoric were accused of 'making the weaker argument appear the stronger', and speakers in the courts took pains to deprecate their rhetorical ability. The originally neutral terms 'sophist' and 'demagogue', which denoted respectively a wise or skilled person and someone influential with the people, took on the negative meanings familiar today thanks to popular distrust of anyone who relied on skill in speaking to achieve his ends.

3-SECOND BIOGRAPHIES
PERICLES
ca. 495–429 BCE
Athenian statesman, highly influential in the assembly

GORGIAS
ca. 485–ca. 380 BCE
Sicilian rhetorician and sophist, famous for ingenious and paradoxical argumentation

DEMOSTHENES
384–322 BCE
Athenian statesman, who employed powerful rhetoric to denounce the ambition of Alexander the Great's father, Philip of Macedon

30-SECOND TEXT
Patrick Finglass

The power of the spoken word was paramount in civic life – from law court speeches to politics, philosophy and drama.

PHILOSOPHY: SOCRATES & PLATO

the 30-second history

3-SECOND SURVEY
The portrayal of
Socrates in the works
of Plato, his most famous
pupil, changed the scope
of philosophy forever.

3-MINUTE EXCAVATION
Plato's Socrates is unusual
because he speaks
positively about women's
intelligence. Although he
shares their ideals, Plato is
not a feminist, concerned
with equality and female
self-fulfilment. In his
Republic, women's
emancipation is embedded
in a complex moral and
political theory where ability
and temperament determine
social roles and education.
Freedom is achieved by
abolishing families because
they threaten social order.
Thus, his means of
obtaining feminist aims
seem repugnant to modern
feminists and liberals.

The death of Socrates, recorded

by Plato and Xenophon, forms the founding myth
of the discipline of philosophy. He defied Athenian
convention by questioning the shared values
underpinning human actions. Socrates conversed
with anyone – young, old, slave, free, rich, poor –
whom he could persuade to answer questions
about concepts like truth, piety, justice and
goodness, stunning them into realizing their
own ignorance. His 'Socratic' method meant
questioning without giving answers; writing
nothing, he said ironically that his wisdom came
from knowing that he did not know. In his words,
'the unexamined life is not worth living'. His
students included Plato, an exceptionally wide-
ranging and profound writer and thinker. Plato's
dialogues establish every branch of Western
philosophy. Some feature Socrates demolishing
preconceptions; others explore Plato's own
philosophical commitments. Foremost among
these is his distinction between objects appearing
good, just or beautiful and the conceptual 'Forms'
of Goodness, Justice or Beauty, intellectually
discernible but merely shadowed by worldly
things. Plato urges his readers to transform their
immortal souls through reasoning about Forms,
in order to lead truly good and fulfilling lives. He
founded Athens' first philosophical school in the
'Academy' neighbourhood.

RELATED HISTORIES
See also
ASPASIA
page 44

PHILOSOPHY: ARISTOTLE
page 92

3-SECOND BIOGRAPHIES
SOCRATES
ca. 470/69–399 BCE
One of the founders of Western
philosophy

PLATO
429–347 BCE
Student of Socrates, philosopher
and mathematician

DIOTIMA OF MANTINEA
fifth century BCE
A real or fictitious philosopher
and priestess whose ideas on the
art of love form the basis of the
notion of 'Platonic' love

30-SECOND TEXT
Kelli Rudolph

Plato and Socrates
helped shape the
discipline of philosophy.

PHILOSOPHY: ARISTOTLE

the 30-second history

Aristotle's life and work

exemplifies his claim (in *Metaphysics*) that 'all humans by nature desire to know'. The son of a Macedonian court doctor, he studied in the Academy until Plato's death, when he was hired as Alexander the Great's tutor. Returning to Athens ca. 335 BCE, he founded his own school, the Lyceum. Confronted with an unknown object, Aristotle says a full explanation will answer (1) what it is, (2) what it's made of, (3) what made it and (4) what it's for (i.e. its purpose: *telos*). Aristotle's interest in (1), (2) and (4) is central to his theory of change. For example, steel in knife-form can *potentially* become sharp, and when applied to a whetstone *actually* becomes sharp; thus, it performs its teleological function by cutting well. Aristotle applies these concepts to ethics and politics. Assuming most people wish to live virtuous, fulfilling lives, he proposes a virtue-based ethics, according to which actualizing our rational capacities (rather than focusing solely on honour or pleasure) fulfils our teleological function. Securing happiness is the main aim of Aristotle's political theory. For him, a *polis* must secure human flourishing. Teleology also guides his *Poetics*, where he asserts that learning through purifying the emotions (*catharsis*) is the function of tragedy; this is achieved through depicting universal themes using the power of poetry.

RELATED HISTORIES
See also
THE *POLIS*
page 16

ALEXANDER
page 26

PHILOSOPHY:
SOCRATES & PLATO
page 90

3-SECOND SURVEY
Aristotle stands beside Plato as an intellectual giant. Unparalleled in scope, his theories influenced centuries of Arabic and Western philosophy, and still stimulate philosophical debate today.

3-MINUTE EXCAVATION
For Aristotle, a prolific researcher and writer, philosophy begins in wonder. He created logic, a systematic approach to reasoning, as a tool for scientific and philosophical inquiry, and developed a theory of categories that served as the skeleton for the body of his work on physics, biology, metaphysics, psychology, meteorology and ethics. These two methods have exerted an unprecedented influence on philosophical systems up to the present day.

3-SECOND BIOGRAPHIES
ARISTOTLE
384–322 BCE
Philosopher and scientist

THEOPHRASTUS
ca. 371–287 BCE
Aristotle's successor at the Lyceum. The first botanist and a key source for the philosophical opinions of Aristotle's successors

30-SECOND TEXT
Kelli Rudolph

Aristotle's wide-ranging accomplishments included teaching the young Alexander the Great and forming new insights into the natural world.

LANGUAGE & LEARNING

Aeolian The dialects of ancient Greek spoken in the central Aegean (Boeotia, Lesbos, Thessaly and the corresponding parts of the north-west coast of present-day Turkey).

Arcado-Cypriot An early ancient Greek dialect spoken in Cyprus and the central Peloponnesian region of Arcadia.

astrologer Someone who predicts the future from the positions of the stars and planets.

Attic-Ionic The Greek dialect group containing the dialects of Attica (including Athens) and Ionia (which included Euboea, the central western coast of present-day Turkey and parts of the northern Aegean). The form of Greek that came to be regarded as 'standard'.

Doric A dialect of ancient Greek spoken in the southern and eastern Peloponnese, Crete, Rhodes and parts of the Aegean. Named after the Dorian people, who also gave their name to a style of architecture.

epigraphic Relating to inscriptions, or their study. The word is from the Greek for 'writing on' (a surface).

epitaph A short text honouring the deceased, perhaps on a tomb. The word is from the Greek for 'on a tomb'.

gladiator A swordsman who fought in the Roman arena as a form of entertainment.

gymnasium (plural gymnasia) The place for a town's young men to receive physical and intellectual training. The name comes from the Greek word for 'naked', as athletes exercised and performed in the nude.

Mycenaean Civilization of the late Bronze Age Greek world, ca. 1600–1100 BCE. Named after the impressive palace-centre at Mycenae on the mainland, it also included the occupation of important sites on Crete and other Aegean islands.

papyrus A paper-like writing surface made from the processed pithy stems of the Egyptian marsh plant *Cyperus papyrus*.

Phoenician From the maritime trading culture of Phoenicia, originating on the coast of present-day Lebanon in the first two millennia BCE. The Phoenician alphabet was the inspiration for the Greek alphabet.

phonemic An alphabet or script system which records the basic, irreducible sound units of human speech.

pictogram A pictorial symbol for a word or phrase.

***stele* (plural *stelai*)** An upright stone slab used as a grave marker, boundary marker or surface for inscribed texts.

syllabic A written character that represents a syllable (typically a consonant + vowel combination), as opposed to a phoneme or word.

THE GREEK LANGUAGE

the 30-second history

Part of the Indo-European

family of languages, Greek shares a common ancestor-language with Latin, German, English, Sanskrit and many others. One of the best attested of all known languages, its written records extend from about 1450 BCE down to the present, with the exception of a gap between about 1200 and 800 BCE. Classical Greek was a language of many related regional dialects, the main branches being Attic-Ionic, Doric, Aeolian and Arcado-Cypriot. From the fourth century BCE a 'common' dialect (the *koinê*) began to take their place, but Attic Greek in particular retained considerable prestige; under the Roman Empire the ability to speak and write in that by-now archaic dialect was highly respected. The abundant written record provides evidence for a huge variety of linguistic registers, from the everyday expressions found in papyrus letters, to the mystical, often deliberately nonsensical language found on lead curse-tablets, to the bureaucratic formality of legal inscriptions, to the elaborate archaisms of poetry. As well as its Indo-European inheritance, Greek borrowed words from languages spoken by peoples with whom the Greeks came into contact – the very word 'alphabet', taken from Phoenician, is an example – and other languages borrowed words from Greek in their turn.

RELATED HISTORY
See also
LINEAR B & THE ALPHABET
page 100

30-SECOND TEXT
Patrick Finglass

3-SECOND SURVEY
Our near-continuous records for Greek over more than three millennia offer a unique opportunity to study a language's development over time.

3-MINUTE EXCAVATION
Greek, like Latin, was an inflected language: nouns, pronouns and adjectives took on different endings depending on the word's gender (masculine, feminine or neuter), number (singular, dual or plural) and, crucially, function (whether the word was the subject or object of the verb, or played some other role within the sentence). Verbs, too, had different endings depending on who the subject was, just like in modern Greek and languages derived from Latin.

The wide range of surviving writing gives us an insight into the expressive power of ancient Greek, in many different contexts.

LINEAR B & THE ALPHABET

the 30-second history

3-SECOND SURVEY
The ability to write was
essential for keeping
records and to transmit
and preserve Greek ideas.

3-MINUTE EXCAVATION
Writing was probably a
specialist skill for scribes
in the Mycenaean world.
Once later Greeks had
acquired the alphabet,
reading and writing were
used to record and transmit
a far wider range of ideas,
from functional texts to
literature. Now a huge range
of human thought could be
transmitted across distance
and even over time. Literacy
became much more
widespread – though
education still required
a substantial investment
of time and money, and
therefore remained out of
the reach of many.

The earliest written record of
Greek is preserved in clay tablets using the Linear
B script, found on Crete and at Mycenaean sites
on the mainland. This script has a number of
pictograms for frequently used words – wine,
gold, jar, and so on – but its real power is in the 89
or so syllabic signs that could be written together
to spell out a word (e.g. 'ku-mi-no' for *kuminon*,
or cumin). Most of the surviving texts are lists
of commodities and objects in the royal palace
storerooms; if the Mycenaeans used Linear B to
write literature, it does not survive. When the
Mycenaean civilization collapsed around 1200 BCE,
the art of writing was forgotten in the ensuing
'dark ages'. As the Greek world recovered,
increasing overseas trade in around the eighth
century BCE brought Greeks into contact with
the Phoenician alphabet (the word comes from
its first two characters, aleph and beth, which
became Greek alpha, α, and beta, β). This
versatile phonemic writing system was a good
fit for the Greek language. Various regions made
small alterations to suit their own dialects, but by
about 370 BCE the version called 'East Ionic' had
become universal and recorded every type of text
from inscriptions to poetry.

RELATED HISTORY
See also
THE GREEK LANGUAGE
page 98

3-SECOND BIOGRAPHIES
SIR ARTHUR EVANS
1851–1941
British archaeologist who
excavated Knossos and
discovered many examples of
the Linear A and B scripts,
which he named

MICHAEL VENTRIS
1922–1956
British architect and linguist who
deciphered Linear B and showed
that it was an early form of Greek

30-SECOND TEXT
Matthew Nicholls

*Linear B used
pictograms for common
words such as gold and
wine, centuries before
the development of the
Greek alphabet.*

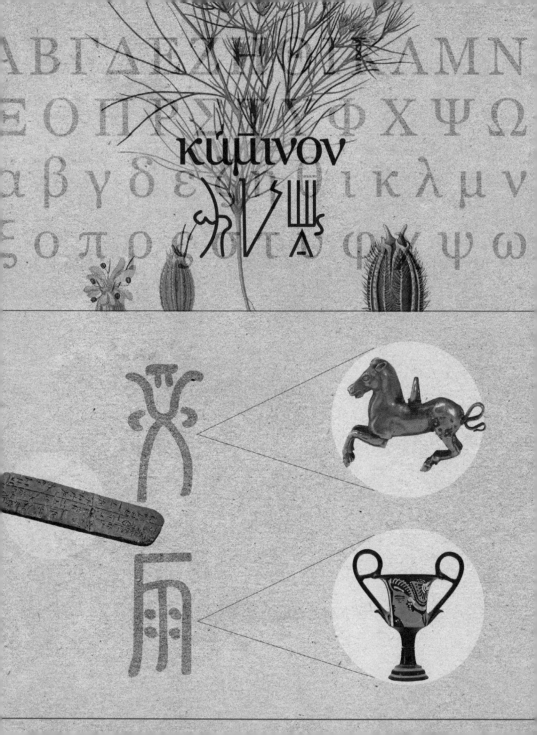

BOOKS & THE LIBRARY AT ALEXANDRIA

the 30-second history

The earliest surviving Greek

writing is on pottery, but the Greeks soon began writing in ink on sheets of papyrus 'paper', made from a widely exported Egyptian marsh plant. The papyrus scroll, widely depicted on vases and in statues, became the standard form of Greek book by around 500 BCE. Sheets glued together and wound round a central boss made a handy, relatively durable and compact vehicle for literary writing. The Greek word for it is '*biblion*', after a Phoenician city where papyrus was traded, giving us words including 'Bible' and 'bibliography'. The typical length of the scroll book form, 1,500 lines or so, may have influenced the way authors shaped or divided their works. By the fifth century BCE there was a book trade in Athens. By the fourth century figures like Aristotle depended for their research on huge book collections, and in the early third century the Greek kings of Alexandria founded their famous library. Here scholars compiled and edited new critical editions and commentaries on important texts, and compared, classified and categorized the (Greek) world's knowledge. Though the founding texts of Greek literature, Homer's poems, had originally been performed orally, the book now dominated Greek literature and scholarship.

RELATED HISTORIES
See also
PHILOSOPHY: ARISTOTLE
page 92

THE GREEK LANGUAGE
page 98

LINEAR B & THE ALPHABET
page 100

3-SECOND SURVEY
The book was the essential medium for Greek literature, allowing authors to read widely and bring their own works to distant audiences.

3-MINUTE EXCAVATION
Books were firmly established by the fifth century BCE in Athens, which is where most of our evidence comes from. They are often shown on vases and are mentioned as part of the everyday backdrop of life in comic plays, which also seem to assume a fair degree of familiarity with the 'literary classics' of the day. Authors even mocked those who bought their books for showing off, rather than for reading. Later Hellenistic kings sought prestige through rival royal book collections.

3-SECOND BIOGRAPHIES
PTOLEMY II PHILADELPHUS
308–246 BCE
King of Alexandria, founded the city's great library

CALLIMACHUS
first half of 3rd century BCE
Poet and author of the Alexandrian library's *Pinakes* (catalogue) – an ambitious classification of all of Greek literature

30-SECOND TEXT
Matthew Nicholls

Books on scrolls of papyrus transmitted and transformed Greek literature, and filled the shelves of libraries like Alexandria's.

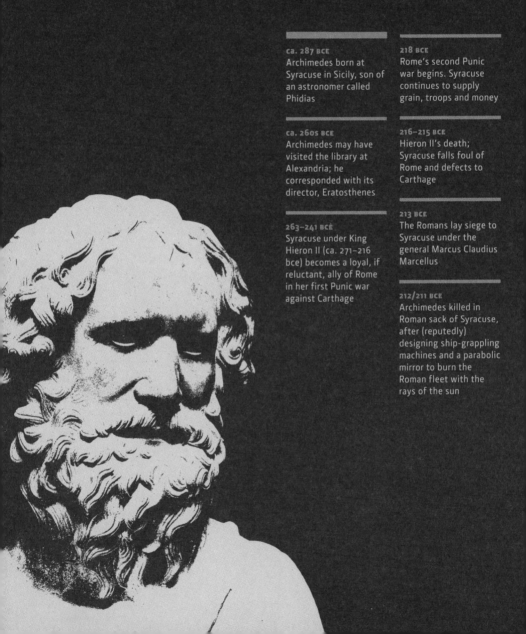

ca. 287 BCE
Archimedes born at Syracuse in Sicily, son of an astronomer called Phidias

218 BCE
Rome's second Punic war begins. Syracuse continues to supply grain, troops and money

ca. 260s BCE
Archimedes may have visited the library at Alexandria; he corresponded with its director, Eratosthenes

216–215 BCE
Hieron II's death; Syracuse falls foul of Rome and defects to Carthage

263–241 BCE
Syracuse under King Hieron II (ca. 271–216 bce) becomes a loyal, if reluctant, ally of Rome in her first Punic war against Carthage

213 BCE
The Romans lay siege to Syracuse under the general Marcus Claudius Marcellus

212/211 BCE
Archimedes killed in Roman sack of Syracuse, after (reputedly) designing ship-grappling machines and a parabolic mirror to burn the Roman fleet with the rays of the sun

ARCHIMEDES

'Eureka!' shouted Archimedes as he ran naked through the streets of Syracuse, giving the world the protoype of the absent-minded scientist. The word means 'I have found it' in Greek; what Archimedes had found was the solution to a problem posed by his friend and patron King Hieron II. The king worried that he had been tricked by the maker of an elaborate gold crown: was it pure gold, or had there been a fraudulent addition of a baser metal? It was easy enough to weigh the crown, but Archimedes needed to measure its volume to work out whether its density was right for the supposed quantity of gold, and this was impossible for such an intricate shape. Watching the water slop over the edge of his bathtub as he got in, Archimedes realized that he could measure the volume of water displaced by the crown to gauge its volume, and it was this original 'eureka moment' that sent him running through the streets in excitement.

Archimedes was given this task because of his reputation as a polymathic inventor and mathematician. He developed a planetarium and a screw device for raising water, and worked with levers; his practical skills were also put to use at the end of his life inventing military machines to repel the Roman siege of his home city.

His greatest and most lasting achievements, however – and, according to the ancient sources, the ones of which he was most proud – were in the loftier field of mathematics. These included geometric works, such as ways to calculate the surface area and volume of spheres, and development of ways to study the properties of floating bodies (hydrostatics). He also developed a system for expressing vastly larger numbers than Greek thought was used to; his book on the subject is called *The Sand-Reckoner*, as he uses the method to calculate the notional number of grains of sand that would fill the universe.

Accounts of Archimedes' death in the Roman sack of Syracuse suggest that the victorious Roman commander did not want him killed; Plutarch recounts that a furious soldier murdered him when he refused to stop working on a mathematical problem, or perhaps when his collection of mathematical instruments was mistaken for treasure.

Matthew Nicholls

INSCRIPTIONS
the 30-second history

3-SECOND SURVEY
Historians speak of the
Greeks' 'epigraphic habit':
their tendency to leave a
written record of events
great and small.

3-MINUTE EXCAVATION
We do not know how
many people in the ancient
Greek world could, or did,
read these inscriptions.
Literacy rates are hard to
determine, with estimates
of 20–30% at the upper
end of the scale. The display
of inscribed texts had a
symbolic value, however,
exposing their contents in
public as a 'guarantee' of
their validity – even if
people did not often stop
to read them.

Public and private displays of
text were everywhere in the Greek world – on
buildings, statue bases, coins, pots and grave
stelai, carved in stone, cast in bronze, and no
doubt painted on biodegradable materials now
lost to us. There are innumerable types of
inscribed text, from simple epitaphs to decrees,
laws, religious dedications, honorific texts
describing the subjects of portrait statues, and
more. They provide a wonderful resource for the
historian, balancing out our literary sources with
functional texts transmitted directly from
antiquity. These texts can take some effort to
decipher. They are often fragmentary or eroded,
and even when perfectly preserved, Greek
inscriptions were generally carved in capital
letters with no punctuation or word breaks to
assist the reader. When collected and read,
these inscriptions can tell us a lot about the
ancient Greek world, covering subjects beyond or
beneath the notice of our literary sources – names
and brief biographical details from thousands of
ordinary tombstones, the operation and structure
of Greek law, how religious sites regulated
themselves and their festivals, the part religion
played in civic life, the running of gymnasia, the
taxation and regulation of trade, how prominent
figures were honoured by their communities, and
much else.

RELATED HISTORY
See also
THE GREEK LANGUAGE
page 98

3-SECOND BIOGRAPHIES
TETTICHUS
second century BCE
'A good man, who perished
in war and lost his fresh
youthfulness', subject of
the earliest surviving epitaph
from Athens

DIOGENES OF OENOANDA
second century CE
Epicurean philosopher who
inscribed a series of philosophical
texts on an 80m (260ft) wall in
his hometown in modern Turkey

30-SECOND TEXT
Matthew Nicholls

*On coins and pots, on
funerary monuments,
and on civic and
religious structures,
inscribed writing
formed part of the
backdrop of Greek life.*

MATHEMATICS

the 30-second history

The Greeks made lasting

contributions to mathematics in a number of fields. Influenced in part by neighbouring Egyptian and Babylonian traditions, Greek theoretical mathematicians developed the distinctive goal of establishing deductive proofs of universal statements written in a step-by-step, logical way: in this they are recognizably in the same tradition as modern mathematics, while their interest in proof, argument and systematic intellectual exploration also brought them into contact with contemporary philosophy. The origins of Greek mathematics are lost to us, though we have the names of shadowy sixth-century BCE figures like Thales and Pythagoras. Euclid's *Elements* (early third century BCE), the earliest surviving written synthesis of what was by then a rich tradition, remained a standard textbook for two millennia: it summarizes a wide range of plane and solid geometry, number theory, irrational numbers and more. Later mathematicians such as Archimedes, Apollonius and Ptolemy built on these foundations, developing more complex geometrical and trigonometrical work and the ability to work with enormously large numbers. A parallel tradition of applied mathematics included work on sundials and water clocks, architecture, engineering and mapping.

3-SECOND SURVEY
The Greeks' impact on the world of mathematics can still be felt today.

3-MINUTE EXCAVATION
The Romans were less interested than the Greeks in pure mathematics, though their surveyors, engineers and architects depended on practical applied maths. It was the Arabic tradition that kept Greek mathematics alive until its rediscovery in the Renaissance, with many Greek works on maths (as well as medicine and philosophy) translated into Arabic from the ninth century CE.

RELATED HISTORIES
See also
ARCHIMEDES
page 104

TECHNOLOGY & ASTRONOMY
page 110

COLUMNAR ORDERS
& MARBLE
page 120

3-SECOND BIOGRAPHIES
PYTHAGORAS
ca. 570–500/490 BCE
Mathematician and religious mystic from Samos, to whom are attributed discoveries in geometry and musical harmonic theory

PTOLEMY (CLAUDIUS PTOLEMAEUS)
ca. 100–170 CE
Mathematician, astronomer and geographer

30-SECOND TEXT
Matthew Nicholls

Greek mathematicians such as Euclid and Pythagoras found new insights into abstract maths and applied fields like astronomy.

TECHNOLOGY & ASTRONOMY

the 30-second history

3-SECOND SURVEY
The Greeks were capable of impressive technological achievements, though some attained only niche interest rather than widespread adoption.

3-MINUTE EXCAVATION
Scholars have tended to argue that intensification and proliferation, rather than real innovation, marked the history of Greek (and Roman) technology. Cultural or social barriers (such as the abundance of slave labour) are often cited as holding back real technological change. However, recent work tries to broaden the narrow view handed down by our literary sources, pointing to some remarkable ancient technological innovations, and to the pride in artisan work shown on many tombstones.

Studying Greek technology can be difficult. A handful of ancient authors talk about technological advances, but many others are uninterested in or prejudiced against artisanal achievements: ancient attitudes to technology and its uses were very different from ours. The archaeological record preserves only a tiny proportion of what must once have existed. Against a backdrop of relative technological stability certain astounding inventions stand out, especially from the Hellenistic age of warfare, expansion and royal competition. In the literary record we have Heron of Alexandria's interest in devices worked by compressed air, steam and water power, while archaeological finds include the Antikythera mechanism. This amazing device of toothed bronze gears can be reconstructed as a sophisticated mechanical astronomical model, designed to show the position of planets and the dates of eclipses on a series of dials. Its construction relied on both a very detailed astronomical and mathematical understanding of the movement of the heavens, and the ability to reproduce it in a finely made mechanism. Though Greek technology may have been characterized more by intensification of existing techniques than by great leaps of progress, tantalizing finds like this suggest that the ancient world may have been capable of more than we know.

RELATED HISTORIES
See also
TRADE & THE ECONOMY
page 52

BOOKS & THE LIBRARY
AT ALEXANDRIA
page 102

ARCHIMEDES
page 104

MATHEMATICS
page 108

3-SECOND BIOGRAPHIES
CTESIBIUS
fl. 270 BCE
Inventor in Alexandria who made a water clock, siege engines and the first pneumatic devices

HERON OF ALEXANDRIA
fl. first century CE
Mathematician and inventor whose work details numerous devices including siphons, pulleys and a sort of (toy) steam engine

30-SECOND TEXT
Matthew Nicholls

The Antikythera mechanism was an amazingly complex and delicate device.

MEDICINE

the 30-second history

There were many types of healing in the Greek world, from astrologers and dream-interpreters to herbalists and amulet-sellers. However, there were also practitioners of what we would recognize as medicine, treating patients with a systematic use of drugs, surgery and prescriptions of lifestyle and diet. Anyone could call themselves a doctor; there was no organized medical profession with agreed methods and training. Medical knowledge was often disputed, and over time rival schools of thought developed. Standards varied widely, but the Greek world was renowned – as in so many learned professions and arts – for the quality of its finest doctors. Many of these men taught and wrote, and some of their work survives (together with archaeological finds). A body of the earliest surviving medical literature is attributed to the enigmatic fifth-century BCE physician Hippocrates from Cos, including the famous oath not to harm patients or breach their confidentiality. Later Greek doctors built on these foundations; the most famous of them was Galen, who rose from treating gladiators in his native Pergamum to the post of doctor to the emperors at Rome, where he produced an enormous, highly influential body of writing that dominated Western medical thinking until the Renaissance.

RELATED HISTORY
See also
PHILOSOPHY: ARISTOTLE
page 92

3-SECOND SURVEY
The Greek world was noted for its doctors and produced men regarded as the fathers of medicine.

3-MINUTE EXCAVATION
The higher reaches of intellectual medicine approached the realm of philosophy, investigating the nature of the human condition. The composition and function of the body and the nature and cause of disease were investigated, as well as how to effect cures. Galen refined a system of 'humours' found in the Hippocratic corpus, writing of a bodily balance between blood, black bile, yellow bile and phlegm (linked conceptually with the four elements of earth, air, fire and water, and the four seasons).

3-SECOND BIOGRAPHIES
HIPPOCRATES
ca. 460–370 BCE
Father of Greek medicine, to whom a wide range of writing were later attributed

GALEN
129–ca. 216 CE
Greek physician to the imperi court at Rome, and author of huge range of medical treatis

30-SECOND TEXT
Matthew Nicholls

Ancient Greek doctor such as Galen and Hippocrates develop and refined complex understandings of th workings of the hum body, including the theory of the four 'humours'.

ARCHITECTURE & BUILDINGS

ARCHITECTURE & BUILDINGS
GLOSSARY

agora The open space at the heart of most Greek *poleis* (cities). Fringed with important civic and religious buildings, it served as a marketplace and meeting place for some political activities.

architrave The horizontal beam running on top of a building's columns, below the frieze, cornice and roof.

capital The element at the top of a column, mediating between the shaft below and the architrave above. The different capital shapes are the easiest way to distinguish the Doric, Ionic and Corinthian architectural orders.

centaur A mythical creature with the head and torso of a human, and the body of a horse. Their legendary battle with the lapiths, portrayed on the Parthenon in Athens, symbolizes the battle between civilization and disorder.

chorus A group of performers who spoke, sang and danced as an extra 'character' in a Greek play, offering commentary and advice on the unfolding action.

chryselephantine A statue with visible parts made of gold and ivory, mounted on a wooden frame.

fluting An architectural term: the grooves, usually vertical, on the shaft of a column.

frieze An important part of a columnar building's entablature, running above the architrave. The differing decoration of the frieze is another important distinction between the different columnar orders.

gymnasium (plural gymnasia) The place for a town's young men to receive physical and intellectual training. The name comes from the Greek word for 'naked', as athletes exercised and performed in the nude.

Hellenistic The period in the Greek world following the Classical era, and preceding the dominance of the Roman Empire. Conventional dates run from the death of Alexander the Great in 323 BCE to the battle of Actium in 31 BCE.

herm A type of sculpture common in Greek cities, especially at crossroads. Consisted of a head or bust on a square pillar base, sometimes with male genitalia. Considered sacred symbols of good fortune, warding off evil.

megaron The principal royal hall of a Greek palace complex. An early form of impressive, often columnar, architecture.

metope A rectangular panel alternating with triglyphs in the frieze of a Doric temple. Often decorated, most famously in the case of the Parthenon in Athens.

Mycenaean Civilization of the late Bronze Age Greek world, ca. 1600–1100 BCE. Named after the impressive palace-centre at Mycenae on the mainland, it also included the occupation of important sites on Crete and other Aegean islands.

Panathenaic festival A four yearly festival held at Athens in honour of the city's patron goddess Athena. Included athletic games, religious processions and sacrifices, and poetry and musical competitions.

Panhellenic Involving all Greek ('Hellenic') communities. The adjective is especially associated with the four great athletic festivals of the ancient Greek world, at Olympia, Delphi, Nemea and Isthmia.

polis (plural poleis) The *polis*, or city-state (with surrounding territory), was the essential political unit of the ancient Greek world, with its own citizen body and legislative structures.

prytaneion A public building acting as a town's seat of government, residence for its officials, home for its sacred hearth and centre for other important symbolic and practical functions.

sanctuary An enclosure set aside for religious purposes, sacred to a particular god or gods. Contained an altar for sacrifice and sometimes temples or other structures for visitors and officials, including (at some sites) provision for healing, for athletic games or for other activities associated with the sanctuary's deity.

stoa A covered colonnade for various public uses, often flanking a town's *agora*. The Stoic school of philosophy takes its name from one such building in Athens where its founder taught his followers.

symposium Drinking party for Greek men, held in the home, with entertainment ranging from drinking games and flute girls to philosophical discussions.

triglyph The regularly spaced, vertically channeled tablets in the frieze of the Doric architectural order. Often said to be a stylized representation of beam ends from an earlier wooden architecture.

volute A spiral-shaped architectural ornament, found in the capital of the Ionic order of columns.

EARLY GREEK ARCHITECTURE

the 30-second history

3-SECOND SURVEY
From palaces to religious centres, early Greek builders created impressive stone statements of power and wealth.

3-MINUTE EXCAVATION
Fine building is a conspicuously expensive luxury: in particular, dressed stone requires sophisticated craftsmen, expensive transport and equipment, large surpluses of labour and a powerful central authority to design and control the process over a relatively long period of time. In Mycenaean times, kings fulfilled this role; Homer praises cities like Mycenae, home of King Agamemnon, as 'well built' and 'rich in gold'. Later, religious sanctuaries and then city-states took on this commissioning and organizing role, creating architecture designed to impress.

The great palace complexes of the Mycenaean Greek world were both residential and administrative royal centres. The eponymous lions of the Lion Gate in the wall at Mycenae (ca. 1250 BCE) flank a column, a symbol of the king's great palace on the hilltop above. Such palaces included a *megaron* or throne-room complex and storerooms for agricultural products; their hilltop citadels were furnished with stone-built wall circuits, water cisterns and monumental royal tombs. The dark ages that followed the collapse of Mycenaean civilization left very few traces of building, mostly simple mud-brick and wooden structures. As the Mediterranean seaways reopened, the Greeks founded overseas colonies and learned about monumental stone architecture (and the necessary art of quarrying stone) from neighbouring cultures like Egypt. By the eighth and seventh centuries BCE the Greeks were building on a grand scale again, this time investing the most effort and expense into temples: palace culture had disappeared, but religious sanctuaries were becoming important centres of wealth and prestige. Early wooden temples, now lost, gave way by the early sixth century BCE to stone and then marble buildings of ever-greater scale and sophistication, as the columnar orders evolved into their canonical forms.

RELATED HISTORIES
See also
COLUMNAR ORDERS
& MARBLE
page 120

SACRED ARCHITECTURE
page 122

30-SECOND TEXT
Matthew Nicholls

Early Greek architecture, such as the palace and Lion Gate at Mycenae, spoke of royal power and prestige.

COLUMNAR ORDERS & MARBLE

the 30-second history

3-SECOND SURVEY

Greek architects used the proportion and style of columnar orders, often carved in fine marble, to create stately, rhythmic buildings.

3-MINUTE EXCAVATION

Ancient architectural theorists felt that the sturdy Doric order was appropriate to major gods, especially male ones, with the later, more slender Ionic (with its fluting and curling, hair-like 'volutes') better suited to female deities. Over time columns began to be used for decorative as well as structural purposes, until by Roman (and modern) times the orders were used in radically ornamental, non-functional ways that might have puzzled Classical Greek architects.

Greek temple architecture has a timeless visual appeal – sturdy, elegant, well-proportioned. This is no accident: it was grounded in the robust 'visual grammar' of the columnar 'orders', conventions of proportion and shape that defined various elements of the building. Each order consisted of a type of column with its associated superstructure, expressing the structure of the building as the column shafts transmit the weight of the roof down into the foundations. The solid, 'masculine' Doric order most widely used in Greek temples typically had a height of six to seven times the diameter of the column base, with a simple top element (capital) carrying a plain horizontal beam (architrave) and a frieze of alternating panels (metopes) and grooved elements (triglyphs). It is sometimes suggested that these elements descend from vanished earlier, wooden buildings. Over time, more graceful and decorative orders (Ionic, Corinthian) were added to the repertoire. The development of this more decorative architecture relied on the abundant supplies of excellent marble available in the Greek world, relatively easily worked and capable of being carved to a fine edge. The Parthenon in Athens, for example, owes much of its splendour to the use of crystalline white marble from nearby Mount Pentelicus.

RELATED HISTORIES

See also
SACRED ARCHITECTURE
page 122

PHIDIAS
page 124

3-SECOND BIOGRAPHY
VITRUVIUS
fl. late first century BCE
Roman architectural writer, whose account of the columnar orders is based on lost Greek predecessors

30-SECOND TEXT
Matthew Nicholls

The different columnar orders, Doric, Ionic and Corinthian, form the basic 'units' of much Greek architecture.

SACRED ARCHITECTURE

the 30-second history

3-SECOND SURVEY
Religious sites were of tremendous importance in the Greek world – not only for worship, but also as places for meeting and for athletic games.

3-MINUTE EXCAVATION
Sanctuaries could be simple, natural places – a spring, a cave, a grove. But the reputation and power of some sanctuaries made them very wealthy, sophisticated places. For example, the prophetic priestess at Delphi, the Pythia, was consulted before a state or ruler carried out any major activity, such as declaring war. This, and visits from humbler individual petitioners, gave Delphi enormous power and wealth over the centuries, which is still visible in the remains of its many splendid buildings.

The Greek temple, with its columns and pitched roof, is one of the most enduring images of Classical civilization. These enormous stone buildings show the importance (and wealth) of religious cults. However, the temple – a house for a god's statue and treasures – was only one element found in the many religious 'sanctuaries' of the Greek world. These sites, sacred to one or other god, consisted of a sacred enclosure (*temenos*) and an altar for sacrifice. Within the *temenos* might stand a temple, a place for ritual offerings and other elements appropriate to the particular god and activities of the site – a sacred spring, a theatre or a space for the healing of the sick. Some of the larger sanctuaries acted as common meeting places for the many Greek city-states, housing not only religious structures, but also stadiums, treasuries and other public buildings. These special sites included Delphi, with its famous oracle of the god Apollo, and Olympia, sacred to Zeus; both were homes (along with Nemea and the Isthmus of Corinth) of 'Panhellenic' games. Rival states and rulers gradually filled such sites with elaborate architectural expressions of their power, under the guise of pious offerings to the gods.

RELATED HISTORIES
See also
GODS
page 58

ORACLES
page 68

PANHELLENIC FESTIVALS
page 70

COLUMNAR ORDERS
& MARBLE
page 120

3-SECOND BIOGRAPHY
KING PYRRHUS OF EPIRUS
319–272 BCE
Rebuilt the sanctuary of Zeus at Dodona as a political gesture of power

30-SECOND TEXT
Matthew Nicholls

Ancient religious sanctuaries such as Delphi adorned majestic natural sites with the rationality and order of Greek architecture.

ca. 490 BCE
Phidias born

ca. 470s BCE
Studies under the sculptors Hegias and Hegaladas

447–438 BCE
Completion of Parthenon under Pericles, by architects Ictinus and Callicrates

438 BCE
Dedication of chryselephantine statue of Athena Parthenos at Athens

438 BCE
Possible embezzlement trial of Phidias, who flees Athens

430s BCE
Dedication of chryselephantine statue of Zeus at Olympia

ca. 430 BCE
Phidias dies

PHIDIAS

Ancient critics like Pausanias and Pliny acclaimed Phidias as the finest of the Classical sculptors, and later artists looked to him for inspiration, though no certain work of his survives. Phidias is famous chiefly for his work in his native Athens at the height of its power and wealth. As the son of a sculptor (Charmides), and a friend of the politician Pericles, he was well placed to help turn the revenues from Athens' tribute-paying empire into a permanent expression of the city's power and splendour.

Phidias was made *episcopus* or overseer for the sculptural programme of the great temple to Athena on the Acropolis, the Parthenon (ca. 447–438 BCE). The rich and unified decorative programme he designed included the famous metopes, with battle scenes between mythical lapiths and centaurs, the great Panathenaic processional frieze, and the pedimental sculpture groups. He also created the giant, 12m (39ft) statue of Athena Parthenos, Athens' patron goddess, which stood in the temple's inner sanctuary. This statue has long since disappeared, but was so famous in antiquity that detailed descriptions (and miniature copies, as shown here) give us a good idea of its appearance.

It was a 'chryselephantine' statue, one of the most prestigious and expensive types of sculpture. Built on a wooden framework, with the flesh of her arms and head carved in ivory and her drapery covered in more than a ton of gold, the statue was an awe-inspiring tribute to the power not only of the goddess, but also of her favoured city.

Leaving Athens under the cloud of a financial scandal, Phidias also produced work for other sites, including most famously the giant seated statue of Zeus at Olympia, one of the wonders of the ancient world. Remains of his sculptural workshop have been discovered there, adding to the literary descriptions of the statue and images preserved on coins and vase paintings.

There are conflicting reports of Phidias' death; Plutarch says that he died in prison on charges of embezzlement (perhaps politically motivated by his closeness to Pericles), while Philochorus says that he was killed after finishing his statue of Zeus. His influence lived on, however, in the work of his pupils in the next generation of Classical sculptors, and in the innumerable copies of his statues made all over the Greek and Roman world.

Matthew Nicholls

TOWNS

the 30-second history

Approaching a city like Athens,

which grew to around 150,000–200,000 inhabitants in the fifth century BCE, a visitor might have passed from farmland through the large Ceramicus cemetery at the edge of the town. Entering through a gate in the city walls – built in the immediate aftermath of the Persian Wars in 478 BCE – our visitor would have passed down winding, irregular streets of packed earth or gravel, lined mostly with mud-brick houses with tile roofs. Here and there he might spot shrines and, especially at crossroads, male statue busts called herms. At the core of the city stood the central public space or '*agora*', which functioned as town square, marketplace and venue for various public ceremonies and events. Religious buildings – including temples and altars – stood at the edges of this space, as well as on the Acropolis that loomed above the town. Many other ancient cities shared these basic features and irregular, organic layout. However, the founders of new colony cities had a chance to try more regular, planned layouts. Right-angled grids of streets accommodated the standard suites of public buildings and private dwellings in a more orderly, regular way that became particularly popular in the late Classical and Hellenistic periods.

RELATED HISTORIES
See also
HOUSES & PALACES
page 128

CIVIC ARCHITECTURE
page 130

ENTERTAINMENT
ARCHITECTURE
page 132

3-SECOND BIOGRAPHY
HIPPODAMUS OF MILETUS
fifth century BCE
Famous Greek town planner, known for his grid plan layouts.

30-SECOND TEXT
Matthew Nicholls

3-SECOND SURVEY
Though individual monuments can be eloquent, the layout and streetscape of ancient cities also tell us a lot about them.

3-MINUTE EXCAVATION
The public-realm infrastructure of a city – streets, water supply and so on – can tell us much about the social and political priorities of its inhabitants. New towns were attracted to regular grid plans both because they symbolized order and rationality, and also because they were relatively straightforward to lay out and promised conspicuously equal shares to would-be settlers. Later the grandiose capitals of the Hellenistic kings took civic planning and building to dizzying heights – influencing their eventual Roman conquerors.

Whether 'organic' and unplanned, or laid out as regular grids, Greek towns tended to contain similar basic features and buildings necessary to the Greek way of life.

HOUSES & PALACES

the 30-second history

Housing in the Greek world – like anywhere – varied according to local climate and building materials, the status and wealth of the owners and the changes of fashion. However, a fairly stable typical Greek design of house can be identified, from excavation in places like Olynthus and from literary sources. Such one- or two-storey houses were private and inward-looking, with rooms opening off a small courtyard (often with a well or cistern for water) and few windows or doors to the world outside. Most were of simple mud-brick with plaster walls, perhaps painted, and had floors of beaten earth. Often the best decoration and furniture was reserved for the *andron*, or 'men's room', a reception room for symposium guests; elsewhere in the house were women's quarters and sleeping space for free and slave inhabitants. Richer houses could afford greater ornament and luxury, from pebble mosaics and better quality wall-painting up to marble columns and water features in the great Greek cities of the Roman empire. The very grandest residences were the palaces of the Hellenistic kings, with monumental architecture and dining halls inspired in part by what Alexander the Great had seen in his Persian and Egyptian conquests.

3-SECOND SURVEY
Home is where the hearth was – the Greek house was the centre of life for the extended family.

3-MINUTE EXCAVATION
Houses help reveal the structure of a society. Legal speeches show the importance – especially when households included slaves and other dependents beyond the nuclear family – of keeping distinct areas of the house for different purposes and inhabitants. Houses were also economic units, helping to process the products of a family's farmland into oil, wool or flour. Xenophon's *Economics* (the word originally means 'running of a household') talks of wives working on textile production and supervising the work of domestic slaves.

RELATED HISTORIES
See also
HOME LIFE
page 46

COLUMNAR ORDERS
& MARBLE
page 120

PAINTING
page 150

3-SECOND BIOGRAPHIES
LYSIAS
ca. 459–380 BCE
Athenian courtroom speechwriter whose legal speeches reveal life inside the Greek house

XENOPHON
born ca. 430 BCE
Greek soldier and writer whose works included the dialogue *Oeconomicus*, or *Economics*

30-SECOND TEXT
Matthew Nicholls

Greek houses served many purposes, from the humble processing of agricultural products to luxury display and entertainment.

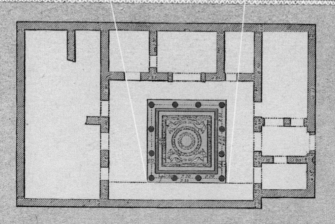

CIVIC ARCHITECTURE

the 30-second history

Greek cities depended for their daily functions, and their sense of shared identity, on spaces for civic activities. The simplest were open assembly places like the Agora or Pnyx hill in Athens, but there were also several specialist building types. The columnar style of Greek architecture first developed in temples was endlessly adaptable to other sorts of building. Over time the public and commercial space at the heart of Greek cities, the *agora*, was ringed with (and in Roman Athens, subsequently filled with) public structures: a mint, fountain houses, council chambers, archives, *prytaneion* (in Athens an office and dining room for magistrates) and more. One particularly important type of civic building was the *stoa*, a long rectangular roofed building of one or two storeys with an open colonnade on one side. This was adaptable to many purposes, from judicial and political activities to philosophical teachings (which is why the Stoic school of philosophy is so called: their founder Zeno taught his followers in Athens' Painted *Stoa*). Towns under the Hellenistic kings developed these loose collections of individual buildings into more systematically planned groups of courtyards, terraces and colonnades, often to striking visual effect. These cities impressed their Roman conquerors and exerted a great influence on Roman architecture.

3-SECOND SURVEY
Greek towns and cities aspired to a range of impressive civic buildings.

3-MINUTE EXCAVATION
A self-respecting Greek town needed more than houses and places of commerce. Pausanias is dismissive of the town Panopeus, 'If one can give the name of city to those who possess no government offices, no gymnasium, no theatre, no marketplace, no water descending to a fountain, but live in bare shelters.' A suite of civic buildings allowed a town to come together in the collective activities of the *polis*, and to express its prosperity and sophistication.

RELATED HISTORIES
See also
CITIZENS
page 42

COLUMNAR ORDERS
& MARBLE
page 120

TOWNS
page 126

3-SECOND BIOGRAPHY
PAUSANIAS
ca. 125–180 CE
Writer whose descriptions of Greek towns are a precious source of information

30-SECOND TEXT
Matthew Nicholls

Elements such as long colonnades and the use of cut stone gave the grandest civic buildings a distinctive look.

ENTERTAINMENT ARCHITECTURE

the 30-second history

3-SECOND SURVEY
The people of the Greek town built places for entertainment as well as religion and politics.

3-MINUTE EXCAVATION
The Romans inherited the Greek love of the theatre and made changes to suit their own tastes. Many theatre buildings in the Greek world were given tall, elaborately decorated walls behind the stage, and had their orchestras reduced to half circles. Some even had adaptations made to allow gladiatorial combat or aquatic events – sure signs of a Roman presence. The Greek gymnasium and stadium inspired, respectively, the luxury Roman bathhouse and circus, adapted for the Roman urban culture of 'bread and circuses'.

The Greeks invented, and loved, theatre. Attending a play, perhaps as part of a dramatic festival, brought a large proportion of the *polis* together. Countless sites all over the ancient Greek world, even relatively modest towns, boast remains of impressive stone theatres. The labour and materials invested in these buildings are eloquent testimony to the importance of drama. Greek theatre buildings tended to have a horseshoe-shaped arc of seating, a little over 180 degrees, leaning back against a natural hillside. Tiered rows of seats – made from earth or wood, then dressed stone in later, more elaborate theatres – rose above a circular orchestra where the chorus danced and sang. A low wooden stage stood behind the orchestra, with a simple *scênê* or backdrop behind that (whence our word 'scene'). Other Greek buildings for what we might loosely call entertainment included the long, U-shaped stadium for athletics and equestrian events, so-called because it measured one stade (about 180 m/590 ft) in length. The larger ones, like that at Olympia (home of the Games) could seat thousands of spectators. The gymnasium was a place for wrestling, exercise and physical training: not just entertainment for its own sake, but part of the formation of the young men of the *polis*.

RELATED HISTORIES
See also
GREECE IN THE
ROMAN WORLD
page 30

PANHELLENIC FESTIVALS
page 70

TRAGEDY
page 80

COMEDY
page 82

CIVIC ARCHITECTURE
page 130

3-SECOND BIOGRAPHY
PINDAR
ca. 522–443 BCE
Lyric poet who immortalized some of the winners of the original Olympic Games

30-SECOND TEXT
Matthew Nicholls

The importance the Greeks attached to entertainment is shown by their specialized theatres and stadiums.

amphora A two-handled jar used for the storage and transport of oil, wine and other goods. Distinctive variations in shape help us identify the date, origins and use of surviving examples.

Attalid The royal dynasty that ruled Pergamum in the Hellenistic period, ca. 282–133 BCE. Noted cultural patrons.

baroque An elaborate style of art and architecture, characterized by rich ornament. The term was applied to the grand and complex art of the late seveneenth and eighteenth centuries.

chamber tomb A tomb with a chamber constructed for the housing of the body: often a relatively expensive and high-status mode of burial.

cist tomb A simpler form of tomb than a chamber tomb, consisting of a small 'box' for the body, made up of stone slabs.

Doric The earliest and simplest of the principal orders of Classical architecture, consisting of massive fluted columns with plain capitals, and a relatively simple entablature.

Geometric Name given to a style of pottery produced in the ninth and eighth centuries BCE. Characterized by multiple horizontal bands of abstract 'geometric' decoration such as lines, meanders, zig-zags and other shapes.

Ionic The second of the principal orders of Classical architecture. The columns are proportionally more slender than those of the earlier Doric, and have distinctive capitals with spiral volutes at the corners; the entablature above the columns is freer in form and often more richly decorated.

Kerch style A late form of red-style vase painting, dating to the fourth century BCE, which incorporates some white-painted elements. Named after Kerch on the Black Sea, where several vases of this style were found.

kore (plural korai) Freestanding archaic sculpture of a young woman or goddess, often with elaborate drapery and hair.

kouros (plural kouroi) Freestanding nude archaic sculpture of a young man or god.

kyathos A type of pottery vessel with a shallow bowl and long handle, used as a dipper or ladle.

Parian marble Pure white marble from the island of Paros, prized in antiquity for sculpture.

Protogeometric An early style of wheel-thrown pottery associated with the end of the dark ages in the Greek world, around the eleventh century BCE. Characterized by abstract bands and circle motifs.

sanctuary An enclosure set aside for religious purposes, sacred to a particular god or gods. It contained an altar for sacrifice and sometimes temples or other structures for visitors and officials, including (at some sites) provision for healing, for athletic games or for other activities associated with the sanctuary's particular deity.

stele (plural stelai) An upright stone slab used as a grave marker, boundary marker or surface for inscribed texts.

tripod A three-footed stand for a seat or vessel, closely associated with Greek sanctuaries where they were often dedicated as offerings.

VISUAL CULTURE

the 30-second history

3-SECOND SURVEY
Visual culture pervaded
ancient Greek life,
particularly in the sphere
of religion, through cult
statues, architectural
sculpture and votive
dedications.

3-MINUTE EXCAVATION
The 'anti-tyranny' decree of
the *nomothetai*, lawgivers
of Athens, dating to
337/6 BCE, was published
on a stone *stele* crowned
with a remarkable image of
the female personification of
the female personification of
democracy, Democratia,
crowning the bearded
male personification of
the populace, Demos,
enthroned. The figure of
Demos is found on as many
as 32 such document reliefs
from Athens, most from
the fourth century BCE, and
labelled (with inscriptions
directly on the stone) on
as many as four.

While visual culture in the Greek
world was most prominent in religion –
sanctuaries were littered with statues in all sizes,
styles and media – from the sixth century BCE, it
pervaded many other aspects of life. Images of
gods and heroes decorated architectural spaces,
public decrees on stone *stelai*, vessels made of
metal and ceramic, even furniture, jewellery and
tableware. Artists created personifications of
non-human entities (festivals and geographic
features) for didactic purposes and combined
them with each other, heroes and gods in
allegorical compositions. Vase painters decorated
their wares with images of daily life – athletes,
drinkers, bathers, sellers and customers,
craftsmen and labourers – known as 'genre'
scenes. Some images illustrate historical and
literary events; theatrical scenes are prevalent on
vases produced and painted in South Italy. Few
of the creators of these objects, however, are
remembered by name. They were decorators,
technicians and craftsmen. In Athens' democracy
few were even citizens. Some artists enjoyed an
elevated status, however, after the end of the
democracy, in royal courts. Through the Hellenistic
period increased expenditure on art, academic
interest in past artists and the documentation of
artistic achievements led to the emergence of the
celebrity artist such as Phidias and Lysippus.

RELATED HISTORIES
See also
VASE PAINTING
page 142

ARCHAIC SCULPTURE
page 144

HELLENISTIC SCULPTURE
page 148

METALWORK & JEWELLERY
page 152

3-SECOND BIOGRAPHIES
PHIDIAS OF ATHENS
fl. ca. 460–440 BCE
Athenian sculptor, artistic
director of the Parthenon

LYSIPPUS OF SICYON
fl. ca. 340–320 BCE
Court sculptor and portraitist
of Alexander the Great

30-SECOND TEXT
Amy C. Smith

*Sculptures, paintings,
pottery, metalwork
and artworks, from the
huge to the delicate,
show the ancient Greek
fascination with every
sort of image.*

POTTERY

the 30-second history

Pottery analysis helps us to

reconstruct the functioning of societies, including trade routes, as well as to date and understand archaeological finds. Open shapes were used for mixing, serving and consuming food and drink, while closed shapes were used for storage and transport. Large vases were also used as grave markers and many pots served ritual functions. Baked clay pots are known from the seventh millennium BCE but the potter's wheel was used in mainland Greece in the Early Bronze Age (ca. 2400 BCE). From the Protogeometric period (ca. 1050–900 BCE), shapes became slimmer and better balanced. Decoration also improved, with better glazes and curvilinear patterns that complemented shapes. The ensuing Geometric period, until 700 BCE, witnessed the emergence of the human figure for decoration. The influence of Eastern imports on Greek artists, in shapes, decoration and technique, characterizes the Orientalizing style (eighth–seventh centuries BCE), when Corinth dominated the market with their black-figure vases. When Athens took the lead in the second half of the sixth century BCE, they introduced the red-figure style, later adapted to local shapes and decoration in South Italian fabrics. Hellenistic wares (fourth–first centuries BCE), more decorative than figural, exploited polychromatic, incised and relief decoration.

3-SECOND SURVEY
Pottery, the most abundant material evidence of Greek antiquity, is the basis for the dating of archaeological finds in the absence of datable texts on coins and inscriptions.

3-MINUTE EXCAVATION
Athenians, who took pride in their ceramics, credited their patron goddess, Athena Ergane, with the invention of the potter's wheel. Yet other Greeks made fun of Athenians for drinking out of ceramic rather than metal cups. Some Athenian pots made for export imitated metal shapes, such as the Nicosthenic *amphora* and *kyathos*. Other ceramics were decorated with ribs, stamped patterns and metallic glaze (fired at a very high temperature) that gave the appearance of metal.

RELATED HISTORIES
See also
VISUAL CULTURE
page 138

VASE PAINTING
page 142

METALWORK & JEWELLERY
page 152

3-SECOND BIOGRAPHY
NICOSTHENES
fl. ca. 540–520 BCE
Athenian potter known from his signature on at least 129 vases

30-SECOND TEXT
Amy C. Smith

In the skilled hands of Greek potters, simple clay could be turned into beautiful – and useful – vessels.

VASE PAINTING

the 30-second history

From ca. 1000 to 300 BCE,

Greek-speaking peoples decorated their finest clay vases with figural images of flora and fauna as well as myths, legends and daily life. Many artists decorated their wares in the Geometric style, named for its stick-like, angular figures and geometric patterns. From the middle of the eighth century, particularly in Athens and Corinth, craftsmen began to decorate their vases with Eastern-inspired plants and creatures and then warriors and other mythic figures. The black-figure technique – silhouetted dark figures enlivened with incisions and patches of colourful clay – was dominant until the 520s, when experiments at Athens resulted in the emergence of red-figure. This new technique enabled painters to represent figures in three-quarter view and led to further experiments over the next century in foreshortening, perspective and shading. At the end of the sixth century, artists competed to represent the naturalistic human form. A florid style, enhanced with gold and other colours over white, emerged, while fourth-century Kerch-style vases – popular in the East – added relief decoration to these techniques. Red-figure styles in the western Greek colonies, especially in South Italy, were adapted to suit local tastes but also evidence a continuing enthusiasm for Greek drama and religion.

RELATED HISTORIES
See also
VISUAL CULTURE
page 138

POTTERY
page 140

PAINTING
page 150

3-SECOND SURVEY
Craftsmen in ancient Greece and its colonies, from ca. 1000 to 300 BCE, decorated fine terracotta vases with figural decoration, employing the black- and red-figure techniques but also polychrome scenes, using coloured clay slips on black, red and white surfaces.

3-MINUTE EXCAVATION
The 'paint' on ancient Greek vases was a slip of fine-grained iron-rich clay suspended in water. Painters applied this slip wherever they wanted the surface to be black. After a three-phased firing process the painted parts remained black while the yellow or red of the underlying vase showed on the unpainted surfaces. Black-figure painters created anatomical and other details through incision whereas red-figure painters used lines and blobs of slip.

3-SECOND BIOGRAPHIES
EXEKIAS
fl. ca. 540–520 BCE
Prolific Athenian vase painter and potter who worked in the black-figure style

EUPHRONIUS, EUTHYMIDES, PHINTIAS & SMICRUS:
THE PIONEERS
fl. ca. 520–500 BCE
Pioneered the development of the red-figure style at Athens

30-SECOND TEXT
Amy C. Smith

The evolving styles of vase painting give us an insight into the Greek visual imagination.

ARCHAIC SCULPTURE

the 30-second history

Archaios, the Greek word for old,
gives us the term 'Archaic', for the pre-Classical
period (ca. 700–480 BCE) and the stiff style of its
sculptures, whether in relief or in the round.
The earliest reliefs decorating temples show
processions of animals or riders (at Prinias) or
static figures (at Gortyn) in the Daedalic style,
named for the mythical craftsman, Daedalus.
Later reliefs incorporate narrative, combining
elements of different stories in one scene (on
the Temple of Artemis, Corfu) or across several
friezes (on the Siphnian Treasury, Delphi). *Kouroi*
and *korai*, freestanding statues of nude youths
and dressed maidens offered as gifts to the gods
at sanctuaries or cemeteries, witness Eastern
influence on style and technique and become
increasingly naturalistic. Earlier *kouroi*, such as
Cleobis and Biton, are four-square whereas later
figures, such as Croesus, are more naturalistic in
posture, surface rendering and proportions, thus
more 'in the round'. Nicandrê, a priestess of
Artemis, dedicated a plank-like figure at Delos
that recalls *xoana*, the earliest statues made from
tree trunks. The funerary epitaph of Phrasicleia,
buried in lead with a *kouros*, likens her to
Persephone, wife of the Underworld god, Hades.
Korai found on the Athenian Acropolis exemplify
Ionic and Doric styles in sculpture and dress, and
attest to their original brightly painted decoration.

*The distinctive 'stiff'
poses of statues like
Cleobis and Biton and
Phrasicleia are typical
of Archaic Greek
sculpture.*

ca. 390s BCE
Praxiteles born

ca. 365 BCE
Birth of his son,
Cephisodotus II

364–361 BCE
Highpoint of
Praxiteles' career,
including work on the
Cnidia

353 BCE
Employed as one of
several sculptors to
decorate the
Mausoleum at
Halicarnassus

ca. 330s
Works on the
Mantinea group

ca. 330 BCE
Praxiteles dies

PRAXITELES

The achievements of Classical sculpture – naturalism merged with idealism, not to mention the ability to convey the sensuality of the female form – culminated in the work of the Athenian sculptor, Praxiteles, in the middle of the fourth century BCE. Praxiteles sculpted freestanding statues of personifications and humans, as well as divinities. While his fame came from his statues, especially those of gods, Praxiteles also sculpted reliefs, perhaps some on the Mausoleum at Halicarnassus, in 353 BCE. Reliefs of the satyr Marsyas and the Muses from a statue base in the Letoion at Mantinea (now in Athens) are understood to be workshop pieces, despite Pausanias' identification of them as works of the master.

While hundreds of ancient texts mention Praxiteles, no extant sculpture is securely attributed to him. Neither attributions nor inscriptions identifying him as creator can be taken at face value. Praxiteles and his father, Cephisodotus, passed their names to later sculptors in their family. As in the case of the Mantinea reliefs, perhaps, Praxiteles' name was used for the products of workshop apprentices. So famous was Praxiteles' name, in fact, that it was regularly added to forgeries in Rome.

In 1877 an unsigned marble statue of Hermes feeding grapes to baby Dionysus (shown here) was excavated at the Heraion temple, Olympia, where, in Roman times, Pausanias saw such a statue by Praxiteles. If this Olympia statue is the master's original it is an early example of the crisp, full drapery and soft flesh associated with later Hellenistic sculpture, thus demonstrating Praxiteles' role as a forerunner to the flamboyant Hellenistic style. Its elaborate sandals and unfinished back, however, encourage scholars to take it as the work of an imitator or a Roman copy.

At the high point of his working career – 364–61 BCE according to Pliny – Praxiteles fashioned his most famous statue, an Aphrodite *Euploia* ('Aphrodite of Safe Voyages') out of Parian marble, originally for the people of Cos, but installed at Cnidos. This *Cnidia*, known from copies, exemplifies Praxiteles' S-curve composition. The original apparently epitomized his exquisite surface work in (painted?) marble, although he also worked in bronze. Praxiteles may have modelled the *Cnidia* among other figures after his lover, the courtesan Phryne. When he promised Phryne his best statue, she discovered that he preferred either his satyr or Eros.

Amy C. Smith

HELLENISTIC SCULPTURE

the 30-second history

3-SECOND SURVEY

Hellenistic sculptures reflect the cosmopolitan era (323–31 BCE) in which they were created and the tastes of monarchs, dynasts and merchants who commissioned them.

3-MINUTE EXCAVATION

The Attalid kings of Pergamum erected the so-called Greater and Lesser Attalid monuments, respectively, on the Pergamene Acropolis in the 220s BCE and the south slope of the Athenian Acropolis in the 150s BCE. These monuments illustrated mythological and historical battles that emphasized Pergamum's victories over enemies and its role as the new Athens. They are attested by ancient writers and dozens of copies of sculpted giants, Amazons, Persians and Gauls in museums throughout Europe.

The cultural period from the death of Alexander the Great (323 BCE) to the Roman victory at the Battle of Actium (31 BCE) is called Hellenistic because in this time art was made in Greek style for an increasingly diverse audience across the Mediterranean. Artists used archaism to evoke styles from previous periods, eventually adapting them for aesthetic effect in neoclassical compositions. In new centres of influence – Alexandria, Pergamum and Rhodes – a baroque style, characterized by intricate, grandiose and theatrical compositions, emerged. After 220 BCE the large reliefs on the walls surrounding the Altar of Zeus at Pergamum showed gods thrashing giants with Classical elegance and baroque anguish. The bold, youthful portrait of Alexander the Great glancing up to his father Zeus, created by Lysippus ca. 330 BCE, influenced the style of portraits of Alexander's successors, as well as the portraits of writers, thinkers and, eventually, Roman generals. Under the influence of Rome's Etruscan predecessors, portraits became more naturalistic, such as the Terme Boxer with his wrinkled face, swollen ears, broken nose and scars in inlaid copper. Late Hellenistic sculptors experimented with issues such as disability, gender and drunkenness, as evidenced by the Mahdia hermaphrodites and the Barberini faun.

RELATED HISTORIES
See also
ARCHAIC SCULPTURE
page 144

PRAXITELES
page 146

3-SECOND BIOGRAPHIES

DAMOPHON OF MESSENE
fl. early second century BCE
Neoclassicist sculptor, whose work evokes styles from the fifth to third centuries BCE

CLEOPATRA & DIOSCURIDES
second century BCE
Married couple who, in 138/7 BCE, commissioned and erected a marble portrait of themselves in their house at Delos

AGESANDER, ATHENODORUS
& POLYDORUS OF RHODES
**ca. first century BCE
–first century CE**
Signed the statue groups of Laocoön and his sons, found in the Baths of Titus at Rome, and Odysseus and his companions, from Tiberius' Villa at Sperlonga

30-SECOND TEXT
Amy C. Smith

Dramatic poses and expressions are typical of Hellenistic sculpture.

PAINTING
the 30-second history

Artists achieved fame in the

creation of wall and panel paintings in the sixth–fifth centuries BCE. Their paintings are now almost all lost, so we have to rely on literary descriptions. Pliny tells us that Cleanthes of Corinth pioneered outline sketches, Ecphantus of Corinth introduced monochrome, Eumarus of Athens first distinguished men from women and Cimon of Cleonae developed *katagrapha*, presenting figures in three-quarter view. Vitruvius reports that Apollodorus of Athens developed *skiagraphia*, contrasting light and shade, while Agatharchus of Samos experimented with *skenographia*, introducing perspective to stage designs at Athens. Polygnotus of Thasus developed a system whereby four pigments – red, black, white and yellow ochre – were used in combination. Pigments were mixed with hot wax, burnt into the surface of marble or wood, for encaustic paintings, as exemplified on tomb *stelai* from Demetrias-Pagasae (third century BCE). Tomb interiors contain some of the best preserved paintings, whether in cist tombs like the Tomb of the Diver at Paestum (480 BCE) or chamber tombs at the Royal Palace of Vergina (ca. 330 BCE). By Roman times many of the most famous paintings – like Aglaophon's painting of the statesman Alcibiades – were seen in a *pinacotheke* or gallery on the Athenian Acropolis.

RELATED HISTORIES
See also
VISUAL CULTURE
page 138

VASE PAINTING
page 142

3-SECOND BIOGRAPHIES
PARRHASIUS OF EPHESUS
fl. ca. 520–500 BCE
Prominent member of the Ionic school, particularly skilled in drawing outlines

HELEN, DAUGHTER OF TIMON THE EGYPTIAN
fl. ca. 340–320 BCE
Said to have painted Alexander the Great's Battle of Issus (333 BCE)

APELLES OF COS
fl. ca. 330–310 BCE
Court painter of Alexander the Great (330s BCE)

30-SECOND TEXT
Amy C. Smith

3-SECOND SURVEY
Ancient writers conveyed to Renaissance and later admirers knowledge of the lost achievements of Greek mural/panel painters, only faintly echoed in vase paintings and mosaics.

3-MINUTE EXCAVATION
The people of Cnidus built a *lesche* or clubhouse at the Panhellenic sanctuary of Delphi, from the booty of their victory over the Persians at the Eurymedon (466 BCE). Polygnotus of Thasus, son of Aglaophon, decorated its interior walls with the '*Iliupersis*' or sack of Troy and the '*nekyia*' or descent into the Underworld. Archaeologists found a Cnidian dedication on a supporting wall that identifies the *lesche's* location, although no paintings have been found.

Though much is lost, just enough ancient Greek painting survives to give us a sense of its colours and themes.

METALWORK & JEWELLERY

the 30-second history

Greeks adapted metalwork

techniques from Eastern craftsmen, whose materials they used and styles they imitated. Our best evidence for the importance of jewellery and metalwork – for adornment and display of wealth – comes from literature (in the *Iliad*, for example, Hera seduces Zeus with gold jewels), yet jewels and metalware are found buried in tombs and hoards. Such riches also served as family heirlooms, athletic prizes, gifts for the gods and stores of public wealth. The most elaborate cult statues were chryselephantine, whereby gold and ivory plates were affixed to clay or wooden cores, an adaptation of the *sphyrelaton* technique, consisting of bronze sheets hammered over wooden cores. Bronze-casting, employing clay moulds and wax models, was later used for vessels and statues. Many Classical statues were cast in bronze but later melted down and transformed into weapons, armour and coins. Goldsmiths – admired for their use of a precious material and high standard of artistic achievement – made miniature statues for use as pendants and earrings. Silver was used after the Persian Wars, in the fifth century BCE, especially for coins. After Alexander the Great captured the treasure of King Darius of Persia in 331 BCE, new fashions, motifs and techniques proliferated throughout the Mediterranean.

RELATED HISTORIES
See also
ARCHAIC SCULPTURE
page 144

HELLENISTIC SCULPTURE
page 148

3-SECOND BIOGRAPHIES
THEODORUS
fifth century BCE
Created an emerald intaglio set in a gold ring for Polycrates, the tyrant of Samos

EUAINETUS
fl. ca. 410–390 BCE
Master die engraver who signed dies for the mints at Syracuse and Catania

PYRGOTELES
fl. ca. 350–320 BCE
Gem engraver, one of only three artists allowed to fashion portraits of Alexander the Great

30-SECOND TEXT
Amy C. Smith

3-SECOND SURVEY
Finely wrought metalwork – ranging from jewellery to weapons and goblets – was the privilege of the wealthy, as evoked in literature and manifested in the contents of tombs, particularly in northern Greece.

3-MINUTE EXCAVATION
The most valuable Greek bronze was supposed to have been made at Corinth. According to Pliny the Elder, *aes Corinthiacum*, or Corinthian brass, was a tarnish-resistant metal alloy of copper mixed with gold or silver. The resulting material, *luteum* (with gold) or *candidum* (with silver), or a combination of the two, was supposed to have been more valuable than its constituent parts. Throughout antiquity it was used for statues, vases and other furnishings.

Greek craftsmen produced a huge variety of useful and beautiful metal objects, from blades to fine jewellery.

RESOURCES

BOOKS

*Ancient Greece from Homer to Alexander:
The Evidence*
Joseph Roisman, translations by J. C. Yardley
(Wiley-Blackwell, 2011)

Ancient Philosophy: A Very Short Introduction
Julia Annas
(Oxford University Press, 2000)

Aristotle: A Very Short Introduction
Jonathan Barnes
(Oxford University Press, 2000)

*The Classical World: An Epic History from
Homer to Hadrian*
Robin Lane Fox
(Allen Lane, 2005)

Classics: A Very Short Introduction
Mary Beard and John Henderson
(Oxford University Press, 2000)

The Greek and Roman Historians
Timothy Duff
(Bristol Classical Press, 2002)

The Greeks and the Irrational
E. R. Dodds
(University of California Press, 1951)

The Greeks: A Portrait of Self and Others
Paul Cartledge
(Oxford University Press, 2002)

*A History of the Classical Greek World:
478–323 BC*
P. J. Rhodes
(Wiley-Blackwell, 2010)

A History of Greek Art
Mark Stansbury-O'Donnell
(Wiley, 2015)

Introducing the Ancient Greeks
Edith Hall
(Bodley Head, 2015)

The Oxford Classical Dictionary
Simon Hornblower, Anthony Spawforth
and Esther Eidinow (eds.)
(Oxford University Press, 2012)

The Oxford History of the Classical World
John Boardman, Jasper Griffin and Oswyn
Murray (eds.)
(Oxford University Press, 1986)

Plato: A Very Short Introduction
Julia Annas
(Oxford University Press, 2003)

Plutarch: The Age of Alexander
Timothy Duff and Ian Scott-Kilvert
(Penguin Books, 2012)

WEBSITES

Perseus Digital Library
perseus.tufts.edu
A huge collection of ancient texts in their original
languages and translation, plus many other
resources.

PHI Greek Inscriptions
epigraphy.packhum.org
The Packard Foundation's searchable database
of Greek inscriptions.

Pleiades
pleiades.stoa.org
This open-source gazetteer website gives
scholars, students and enthusiasts worldwide
the ability to use, create, share and map historical
geographic information about the ancient world.

Stanford Encyclopedia of Philosophy
plato.stanford.edu
This continuously updated encyclopedia of
philosophy, written by experts in the field,
contains many articles on ancient philosophers
and the development of their theories.

NOTES ON CONTRIBUTORS

EDITOR

Dr Matthew Nicholls is an ancient historian at the University of Reading, where he works on ancient books, libraries, architecture and cities in the Greco-Roman world. He has a particular interest in the digital reconstruction of ancient spaces (including an award-winning digital reconstruction of ancient Rome). Following the success of his *30-Second Ancient Rome* book in this series, he is delighted to turn to the ancient Greeks.

CONTRIBUTORS

Emma Aston is the Classics Head of Department at the University of Reading. Her first book, *Mixanthrōpoi: Animal-Human Hybrid Deities in Greek Religion* (2011) on the depiction of Greek deities in part-animal form, reflected her interest both in ancient religion and in Greek attitudes towards animals and the natural world more generally. She is now working on a book on ancient Thessaly, a part of northern Greece famous for its cavalry, its witches and its epic heroes (Achilles was born there). Emma enjoys teaching many aspects of Greek history to undergraduates, including agriculture, warfare, religion and the society of ancient Macedon, homeland of Alexander the Great.

Timothy Duff is Professor of Greek at the University of Reading, where he teaches Greek history, literature and language. He is author of *Plutarch's Lives: Exploring Virtue and Vice* (Oxford 1999), *The Greek and Roman Historians* (Bristol Classical Press/Bloomsbury 2002) and *Plutarch: The Age of Alexander* (Penguin 2012), and of numerous papers in scholarly journals and collections. He has held academic fellowships in Berlin, Cambridge, Cincinnati, Harvard, Princeton and the Australian National University, and has taught at the British School at Athens.

Patrick Finglass is the Henry Overton Wills Professor of Greek at the University of Bristol, and a Fellow of All Souls College, Oxford. His main research interests are in Greek tragedy and lyric poetry, and he has published editions of Stesichorus (2014), Sophocles' *Ajax* (2011) and *Electra* (2007), and Pindar's *Pythian Eleven* (2007) with Cambridge University Press. His current project is an edition of Sophocles' *Oedipus the King*.

Katherine Harloe is Associate Professor of Classics and Intellectual History at the University of Reading. Her research interests include the history of Classical scholarship, the history of political thought, the reception of Greek and Roman antiquity in European (especially German) culture before 1945, reception theory and Greek literature. She is author of *Winckelmann and the Invention of Antiquity* (Oxford University Press, 2013), and co-editor of *Thucydides and the modern world: reception, reinterpretation and influence from the Renaissance to today* (Cambridge University Press, 2012).

Kelli Rudolph (AB Princeton, PhD Cambridge) is a lecturer in Classics and Philosophy at the University of Kent, where she specializes in early Greek philosophy and science. She has a particular interest in ancient theories of sensation, and in addition to publications on ancient philosophy, she is also editor of *Taste and the Ancient Senses* (Routledge, 2017).

Amy C. Smith is Professor of Classical Archaeology and Curator of the Ure Museum of Greek Archaeology at the University of Reading. She primarily researches ancient art, particularly vase painting and images of myth, religion and politics. In *Polis and Personification* (2011) and many articles, she has written about the use of personifications in ancient Greece. She has co-edited *The Gods of Small Things* (2011) and Brill's *Companion to Aphrodite* (2010). Professor Smith also studies museum collections both online and offline and has co-edited and contributed to several museum catalogues.

INDEX

ACKNOWLEDGEMENTS

All reasonable efforts have been made to trace copyright holders and to obtain their permission for the use of copyright material. The publisher apologizes for any errors or omissions and will gratefully incorporate any corrections in future reprints if notified.

Alamy Stock Photo/© Heritage Image Partnership Ltd: 61C; © World History Archive: 78BG.

Architect of the Capitol: 19TR.

Flickr/Xuan Che: 107BC; Tilemahos Efthimiadis: 145BC; Matthiasberlin: 145T; Sarah Murray: 145TC; Carole Raddato: 146; Helen Simonsson: 145L, 145R; Ann Wuyts: 101BR.

Getty Images/De Agostini: 31C, 61T; Leemage/UIG: 139C; Print Collector: 103T; Time Life Pictures/The LIFE Picture Collection: 104; ZU_09: 89BL.

The J. Paul Getty Museum/Digital image courtesy of the Getty's Open Content Program: 103B.

LACMA, www.lacma.org: 99B, 153 (bracelet, earrings & bull).

Library of Congress, Washington D.C.: 41BR.

Courtesy National Gallery of Art, Washington: 31BR, 63L.

National Library of Medicine: 113C.

Nick Rowland: map artwork 8.

Shutterstock/Alessandro0770: 51TL & TR; Hintau Aliaksei: 6; Anastasios71: 7T; Anton Balazh: 123TR; Ivan Bastien: 19TL; Radu Bercan: 2BR, 121BR; Cromagnon: 59T; Asaf Eliason: 107T; Eyüp Alp Ermis: 71C; Everett Historical: 41T, 93BL, 93BR; Markus Gann: 2R (2nd from top), 121R (2nd from top); Oleg Golovnev: 133C; Sergey Goryachev: 59C; Leigh Gregg: 119BL & BR; HildaWeges Photography: 64; imagedb.com: 31TL; Marina Kalenskaya: 99C; Kamira: 26; Panos Karas: 7B; Lambros Kazan: 17C; Kert: 131C; Vladimir Korostyshevskiy: 47T; Lazyllama: 133BR; Giancarlo Liguori: 61BL; Lynea: 93TR; Marzolino: 39T (background), 93TCR; MidoSemsem: 17R; Montebasso: 109TR; Paul B. Moore: 11T; Morphart Creation: 19BC, 93TCL; Dmitry Naumov: 69T; NesaCera: 25B; Hein Nouwens: 83B, 93TL; Olemac:

53T (2nd left); Panbazil: 69T; Lefteris Papaulakis: 133BL; PerseoMedusa: 2R (2nd from bottom), 121R (2nd from bottom); Anders Peter Photography: 59B; Paul Picone: 53TL, 53TC, 53TR; Pio3: 23C; Matt Ragen: 123CL; Titania: 21C; Ververidis Vasilis: 21(Main); Haris Vythoulkas: 59CL; Yoeml: 91B; Roberto Zilli: 61BR.

Courtesy of the University of Texas Libraries, The University of Texas at Austin: 25C.

The Walters Art Museum: 23T, 23BC, 51TC, 53T (2nd R), 63R, 73B, 78B, 101CL, 101, 139CL, 139CR, 143 (all images), 153 (cup, coin, goat, mirror, statue).

Wellcome Library, London: 83R (background), 83L (beetle), 87C, 109C, 109BC, 113TR, 113BR, 113 (background).

Wikimedia Commons/DerHexer: 83T; Herbert Josl: 83C (background); Stas Kozlovsky: 63T; Marsyas: 39B; Marie-Lan Nguyen: 11B, 29BL, 41BG, 44, 78T, 81T, 85, 87TL, 91T, 91TL, 93BC, 149TR, 149BR, 151T; Sailko: 29BR; Velvet: 69CR, 115C.